THE SWORD FROM THE SCABBARD

The Buddhist Response to Nihilism

The Sword From The Scabbard

ISBN 978-1-84799-249-9

The Sword From The Scabbard

For my parents, Jim and Rosemary
Thank you for everything

The Sword From The Scabbard

CONTENTS

The Sword From The Scabbard

INTRODUCTION

Most introductions to books begin in some way as kind of apologetic explanations for what is going to follow. This is not really going to be much different. The main point of concern for some readers will be about the criticism levelled throughout this book against certain thought systems or world views. I hope to use this introduction to explain why it is necessary for me to do so.

Essentially this book is about what is commonly known as Buddhism and the impact its teachings can have on both individuals and on the world we live in. In order to do this I am going to explain about its source and some of the details of its description of reality. The main point I am going to try and get across is its highly applicable nature to those living in the world today and the insight it can grant us into the issues of our age.

In order to do this it is important to look deeply into our past and find the roots of some of the issues that are of concern in the West today. It is important to understand the shaping and character of Western society and belief systems in order to understand why the nature of the problems of modern life are the way they are. That is why the book is structured in the way it is. Firstly there is an account of how we got to where we are, then a description of where we are and some of the problems that can be found here. Without this the third part, that concerning Buddhism, would not have the resonance it should. That is why it is necessary to look at some of the thought systems and beliefs that have been found both in Western history and in the world today. That they are discussed in a way that challenges them (or at least the most fundamentalist versions of them) is something that is unavoidable. Without examining the past as honestly as possible we will not be able to understand who we are and why we believe the things we do. Or overcome the mistakes that were made then. What I hope is that none of the criticisms levelled at certain thought or belief systems is mistaken for needless aggression.

This is a short book and so has to be rather basic in all of the issues it concerns. It is hoped that it will give the reader some interest in the issues discussed and that they will look into them deeper for themselves. There is a wealth of literature available on every chapter and almost every topic. The notes and reference system has been laid out in a way that make this easier for the reader to do so if they wish. It should be recognised that what is accounted here, especially chapter 5, is only a glimpse into several areas of research that have been growing over the past few decades and that those who are curious about any of the conclusions or ideas put forward are encouraged to look into these areas of research themselves.

The book begins discussing the Christian heritage of Western civilization and how deeply it has influenced how we have viewed and continue to view the world around us. Then we will look into how and why these views have come under pressure in recent times and the subjects of concern this has given rise to such as the birth of nihilism and the increase in cases of depression. The second half is devoted to explaining the roots and nature of what is known as Buddhism and how it is uniquely able to bring understanding and even a measure of resolve to each of these issues. I hope there is included at least one paragraph that increases the readers understanding of the world around them.

PART ONE

The Sword From The Scabbard

1

SON OF MAN

Many people living in what is commonly understood as the Christian world have realised that their traditional religion has encountered several kinds of difficulties in the emergence of modern times. It has seemed to them that many of the claims of its adherents have been proven hopelessly wrong, primarily through the methodology known as science, and so the Christian analysis and description of reality has been thrown into, at the very least, serious doubt. The once powerful and respected clergy has, because of this, lost most of the esteem it once carried and those who search for knowledge about themselves and the world around them now look to other sources for answers.

It is generally perceived that this issue has formed the emergence of two fears. The first is from those who continue to practise their faith and the apprehension they feel at its erosion. A fear has risen among those involved in the faith that if some of its tenants have been proved incorrect, then it is entirely open to question. In the past this fear was kept at bay by the destruction of any form of heresy. Today this is no longer possible. The other fear that has developed is from those who have rejected this creed in its entirety, mainly because of modern scientific discovery, in that Christianity and other religions are a threat to human progress.

We can see these two fears colliding with each other from watching attempts by what appear to be the two dominant creeds that have developed over the past one hundred and fifty years, scientific atheism and religious fundamentalism, to overcome and undermine one other. An example of this from the Christian side is the teaching of creation science. Much has been written and said, through attempts like this, to stress the rationality and evidence behind fundamentalist Christian belief, but which has inadvertently betrayed some of the central principles of both religion and the scientific method. A lot has also been written in support and defence of total atheism lately, as can be seen across the shelves of the religious section in most of today's bookstores.

Once I met someone who tried to explain to me that evolution was not possible because it breaks the Second Law of Thermodynamics. He also explained to me how Neanderthals were mentioned in the Bible and so can be accepted by the Christian tradition to exist. This kind of picking and choosing from scientific discovery and historical research is counter productive, not only for science, but for the Christian cause as well. The realms of religious faith and scientific practise should not be mixed in such a simplistic manner. Another problem is that creation scientists who take part in such study and research are falling into a debate of which only a small number of believers or disbelievers take part. In many ways this perceived conflict between scientific atheism and religion is coming to be viewed as highly illusory.

The battle line seems to have been drawn by the most fervent atheists of the 19th century and carried through to modern times by their heirs in the form of scientists and writers such as Richard Dawkins and Christopher Hitchin's. Those in this tradition see religion as a primitive and dangerous tradition which humanity needs to cast of in order to develop itself further. Religion can be seen as an emotional crutch or primitive explanation for how the world has developed, soon to be completely undermined by science and a respect for the world it reveals to us. An example of a work in this tradition is Dawkins bestseller *The God Delusion*. Its attack on faith in God and the Christian belief system feels dated and unoriginal and echoes the patronising tone of 19th century atheists. Dawkins work as a scientist is exemplarily as well as groundbreaking and deserves much admiration. His motives for desiring humanity to relinquish religious belief are also probably benevolent, but telling us that fundamentalist Christianity is not an accurate reflection of reality feels somewhat unnecessary.

Most Christians do not respond to attacks of this nature. Some even realise how they are flawed in that they attack what atheists perceive as Christianity rather than how most of its adherents experience it. So called scientific research such as that on Intelligent Design, however, does attempt to counter attack the challenge from a scientific angle of its own. This reveals the shaky foundations of their own faith and exposes them and what they believe to attack from more capable and less ideologically influenced researchers. By placing the foundations of their faith on scientific 'discoveries' they place those foundations under easy attack.

If this conflict between science and religion is being carried out it is being done by only a small number from each side. Not all scientists are atheists or wish to see religion expunged from human experience and not all those who are religious disbelieve the discoveries of scientific research. Those who continue to see themselves as part of this struggle for the future are carrying out debates that for most others feel redundant. Most people have managed to strike up a kind of working balance between the two.

An example of such a redundant debate is that of evolution and the continuing intellectual conflict, most loudly in the United States, which surrounds it. The evidence for evolution and its explanatory power is at the very least highly convincing. Mainstream Catholicism has even accepted it as 'more than just a theory'. If there are people who continue to disbelieve in it, despite the evidence, then no amount of arguing will convince them otherwise. It is not difficult to also see the holes in the counter argument of Intelligent Design. Creationism renamed is not going to win more arguments than creationism did.

Robert Winston's decision not to join Richard Dawkins in condemning certain schools which had decided to teach a form of creationism in their curriculum saw the flaws in this kind of conflict. Although it is an unfortunate sign of the limited mindset of those involved, forcing them by law not to teach what they believe feels unnecessary. He also recognised all of the debts modern secular society owed to its Christian heritage. Debts that made turning around and attacking it in this way feel like unneeded aggression. In time the students at these schools will encounter the current understanding of evolution and choose for themselves. Some will disagree with it but it is doubtful introducing the idea to them at a younger age will alter that outcome.

Any real debate in creation versus evolution is dead. Pinning hopes of religion falling or surviving on its outcome is dangerous for those who do so. Those who argue in support of creationism have shown in many cases to lack a clear understanding of Darwin's hypothesis on the development of life. Statements and questions such as 'If humans evolved from monkeys why are there still monkeys in the world today?' betray a highly anthropocentric and bare conception of the understood mechanisms of evolution. Arguing with one of sciences most successful discoveries to support your cause is dangerous as the evidence supporting it will only continue to grow. Those who use such means to support their faith would be safer focusing on less clearly understood aspects of reality if they are adopting this strategy. Choosing not to believe something which so much evidence has grown in support of is also dangerous because of its contrary approach to the world that surrounds us. It is not an attitude that should be indulged in by those who carry it.

Another kind of debate that feels empty is within the borders of modern Christianity itself. It is today's version of those differences of opinion which helped tear Europe apart during the Reformation. Today, it is still the area of discord that divides the many churches within the Christian tradition. Revolving around various versions of Biblical interpretation and church structure it comes in the form of doctrinal dispute and various degrees of liberalness and conservatism within each church. Today we seem to see this form of debate covering the churches' attitudes towards homosexuality and female ministerial positions rather than the nature of the Trinity or the reality of transubstantiation, as it was in the past.

Many of those who follow or even have strong views in such debates appear as if to be unaware of the much more fundamental issues that are challenging modern Christianity. Within the Islamic tradition there is a word that describes this kind of debate perfectly.

The Sword From The Scabbard

The word is 'zanna' and most accurately refers to pointless theological speculation. This kind of speculation rings pointless because it is not possible to discover real answers from it. Debating the nature of God and the true position of Jesus' mother Mary in his mission are pointless because a satisfying answer cannot be revealed that will convince everyone. In terms of 'zanna', an answer perhaps can also not be revealed because there isn't one or the question itself is in some way inadequate.

It is also disappointing that these are the limits of the areas of debate that those who belong to Western religious traditions see their clergy and ministers engage in. More recent discoveries have opened up insights into the Christian past and the nature of Jesus' mission that would seem a more fitting challenge for church leaders to deal with. What is the point of debating whether Jesus would have approved of women priests if, as it seems, he never intended for a new religion to be formed at all? All of those attempts at trying to discern or explain the nature of the Holy Trinity would be rendered void if, as it also appears, Jesus never claimed to be divine.

All of these are issues that should be addressed but all pale in significance to the problem of the gulf that has opened up in the West between religious officials and members of the public. Today's churches do not seem to have the means or the capability to deal with the specific problems that are afflicting those living in modern society. The only solution to what could be considered as the spiritual problems of nihilism, suicide and self destructive behaviour seeming to be having more faith in God and his plan for the world. This is a remedy many of us find difficult to accept.

Although most people can see the admirable social teachings of Jesus, few do not have any difficulty accepting the metaphysical connotations of regarding him as the Son of God. Literal Biblical interpretation seems to be thrown into this package as well. This is difficult when belief in miracles and an afterlife is something that many people have left quietly behind. Or others attack with contempt.

When spiritual officials in the past have been out of touch with the people they have served it has often been just before or during times of great change. This is easy to see in our own time but is more interesting when considering that conceptions of divinity and spiritual meaning have in the past changed to suit their times. As each generation that has encountered these changes and dismissed the spirituality of their past new conceptions of divinity and the spiritual path have arisen to replace them. This is why modern Christians should consider the gulf between themselves and what is considered mainstream society an issue of the utmost importance.

The history of Western society is swamped in Christianity, an amalgamation of Judaism, Greek philosophy and the pagan world that preceded it. Even those ideological movements that would later develop espousing a communist state or master race owed more to the Christianity they attempted to reject than they would admit. To understand how many living in Western society have come to exist in what has been described as a state of existential boredom or nihilism it is important to understand the chain of events that has led to its emergence. This chain also helps explains the conflict between science and religion and why neither side seems to be capable of gripping the others conclusions about the nature of the world around us and our place within it. Subtle events and opinions in the past have gone on to completely alter the way history has developed and the way in which the world has come to perceive itself.

In an issue of *St. Martins Magazine* a reader once wrote in expressing concerns about the, at that point, new movie *The Da Vinci Code* . Most people who are familiar with this film realise it is based on a bestselling book of the same title. Many critics have attacked it as no more than trash fiction, which mostly it is. It is also, however, an easily read action story with a compelling mystery at its centre. The hero is Robert Langdon, who gets caught up in a murder mystery involving sinister elements within the Catholic Church. They are attempting to suppress a truth about the history of their faith which could be devastating to Christian belief. This truth has been kept alive and remembered by an organisation known as the *Priory of Sion*, which included leaders such as Isaac Newton and Leonardo Da Vinci (Hence the title).

The hidden truth is revealed in the end that Jesus and Mary Magdalene founded a bloodline that continues to the modern day. In the book it leads to none other than the pieces heroine, Sophie. The part that it is assumed so bothered the *St. Martins Magazine* reader was not only the idea of Jesus and Mary Magdalene having sex but also the revelation that Jesus was no more than an ordinary human being. Understandably it puts a slight dampener on any promises of eternal glory or a loving God attributed to him.

The response, by a priest incidentally, reassures the concerned letter writer by quite rightly dismissing much of *The Da Vinci Code* as speculation and nonsense designed primarily to entertain, which is an area in which it does succeed. The idea of a bloodline being tracked successfully for two thousand years directly into one family is incredulous in itself, never mind only one candidate, and the books portrayal of the Catholic organisation *Opus Dei* is perhaps a little too sinister. However, by being wrapped up in fictional garb there is key point reached at by the books conclusions that could almost be dismissed as easily as the rest but for the wealth of evidence that has already been amassed in support of it. It is this piece of truth that the mystery plot is able to build upon to create a modern day bestseller and successful, but lacking, movie. It is understanding properly this particular point that can also lead to an understanding of where modern society has found itself today. Our *St. Martins Magazine* reader would be right to be concerned about this and its implications for how he views his faith. It is a pity only that he has touched upon it in a work of fiction and not from more reliable sources. Or perhaps not, because if that had been the case his doubts would not have so easily been dispelled. This truth concerns the nature of both Jesus and his mission.

An important point to remember is that although we do not know as much about Jesus as was once thought we still know more than nothing, as some strident atheists would have us believe. Although the Gospels cannot be relied upon as complete historical truth they cannot be entirely dismissed either. The fact that there was a man called Jesus is impossible to dismiss. His original name probably would have been Yeshua, which in modern English corresponds to Joshua. The name Jesus may have been derived from the translation of Yeshua into Greek before being translated to other languages.

Factors that must be remembered include that the Gospels were compiled at their earliest forty years after this mans death. It is also helpful to keep in mind that St. Paul, the man attributed more than anyone else with founding Christianity, would never have met the historical Jesus.

In the earliest Gospel, Mark presents Jesus as a more human figure than Christian tradition remembers him. Although glossed over by most denominations, especially Catholicism, we hear about Jesus' brothers and sisters. Although this is clearly contained in *St. Marks Gospel* it often comes as a surprise to those raised as Christians that Jesus had siblings. In the Catholic tradition it casts shadows on the revered image of the Virgin Mary as well as making Jesus appear that little bit more human. Connected to this is the issue that at no point in the Gospels does Jesus claim to be divine. The Doctrine of the Incarnation that would hold him up as the Son of God would not be completed until hundreds of years after his death. It is unlikely even that those who wrote the Gospels perceived him to be the Son of God in the way modern churches do. Interestingly, he referred to himself as the Son of Man, a title seeming to emphasise his humanity more than anything else.

Most of this information can be discerned by reading the New Testament itself. When we begin to look outside it, especially from the tradition Jesus emerged from, more light is shed on the true nature of his mission. What becomes clear during this is the almost completely Jewish nature of his teachings. One of Jesus' most famous sayings is an echo of Rabbi Hillel's teaching about not doing unto others as you wouldn't want done unto you. It would seem that Jesus never strayed too far from the Jewish methods of prayer and conceptions of divinity. It has also been speculated, not without base, that Jesus may have been a part of the Pharisee school, given the great similarities between their teachings.

Judaism, when Jesus lived, was greatly respected by the Romans because of its old age and unique customs. They had developed a conception of divinity as a transcendent God and method of life inspired by making this God a presence in their day to day activities. Various sects developed concerned with the best way in which to live in accordance with this divine presence. The Essenees, for example, rejected mainstream life in Judea and set up base near Galilee, where many of there scriptures would be discovered almost two thousand years later as the Dead Sea Scrolls.

The Jews had, by the time Jesus was born, suffered deeply. Imprisonment in Babylon had been followed with political domination by the Greeks, and then the Romans. Many had developed expectations of a messiah figure to release them from the seemingly perpetual suffering they were condemned to endure. From before Jesus was born this messiah had been expected to release the Jewish people from the rule of the Romans. No one believed he would in some way be divine, which would be considered blasphemy in monotheistic Judaism, but that he would be an individual who God had blessed with great ability.

It has also become increasingly clear that Jesus' early followers never believed he was divine in the way later Christians would. We know this because of how they were permitted by the Jewish authorities to pray in the Temple at Jerusalem after his death. Had he claimed or his followers believed him to be the literal Son of God this would have been impossible because of the rules concerning Jewish blasphemy. Only movements and schools that were considered authentically Jewish were permitted by the authorities to use the Temple.

At a lecture concerned with the historicity of Jesus I noticed the reactions of several of the other audience members who happened to be Christians. Our lecturer was not disguising any of the conclusions that had been reached at and I could see he was making those members of the audience uncomfortable. This in no way is meant to suggest that he should have hidden the results of years of research or somehow made into a more digestible form. What it does show is the highly undermining nature of this kind of research. The Christians in our class, some of whom never returned, were right to feel uncomfortable. The life and teachings of Jesus as the Son of God are the cornerstones of Christian faith. To have that undermined by historical research and applied knowledge is a much greater threat than to have that faith rejected because it sounds unrealistic or even impossible.

For many non-believers the life and miracles of Jesus is just a bizarre mystery or mistake of history that they seek no explanation for. Believers counter this with the explanation that the strangeness of what was recorded can only be explained fully by accepting that Jesus was, in fact, the Son of God. Only then can we understand how he was able to perform the miracles that were reported. Most Christians are familiar only with this kind of disbelief and find their faith intact after dealing with it. They see others blind to what they see and unable to accept the implications of Jesus and his teachings. When dealing with research on the historical Jesus, however, it is not so easy to turn away undisturbed. By comparing details within the Gospels to the wider historical context of the time a much clearer and less supernatural image of Jesus' life emerges. It is the clarity of this other explanation and ones like it that stand it above the traditional Christian interpretation. With the use of comparisons to the various thought systems of Jesus' time his sayings and life resonate with meanings which have been previously lost in history.

What the Gospels appear to be is known as a hagiography; a spiritual biography. This method of recording events is easiest to find in the lives of the Christian saints. It is a biography that mixes the meaning of a person's life with the events that occurred within it. The stories of miracles convey a meaning much deeper than a literal interpretation gives them. Making the blind see can be interpreted as how having faith opens up a new way of seeing the world and so how having faith can be life transforming. To believe it was an actual event that occurred two thousand years ago robs the story of its immediate importance. It was also used as a method to preserve and continue wisdom sayings and traditions that were common throughout many cultures at this time. Some fear that without literal meaning the Gospels have no relevance to people today when in fact the opposite is true. Reading the Gospels and Jesus' words with this meaning freshens them with a deeper and more powerful significance.

Even when Jesus advised his followers to have faith it was not in the sense of having a detailed belief system that is usually attributed to the term today. Having faith meant believing in life with its purpose and meaning despite the evidence of pain and suffering that surrounds us. It also meant cultivating an openness and sense of God within life. In this way Judaism and Jesus' version of it was a deeply life confirming practise. Today faith is often interpreted as believing in the Incarnation or the Christian concept of God. In some worrying cases it has even been understood as the ability to believe in something despite the evidence against it that surrounds an individual.

Jesus is believed to have been crucified in the year 27 CE. There is no doubt that he must have been a highly charismatic and revered figure, to have begun such a following for his brand of Judaism. The huge effect he would have had on the lives of those who joined him made it difficult for them to accept it when he had died. Rumours circulated that he wasn't really dead and that he had risen in a new way to spread his teachings and help his followers. There is a kind of truth in this story in that his teachings, of which he would have considered himself a reflection of, continued after his death. I do not think many Christians, however, would find this interpretation fully satisfying.

Modern Christian theology has placed the literal interpretation of Jesus' resurrection at the centre of their belief system. It is this event that proves his divine nature and power over death. His resurrection is considered the prototype for the resurrection that awaits all true believers in his message. Again, like the Incarnation, this doctrine would take centuries to be formulated. Jesus' earliest followers would not have imagined such an otherworldly version of their teacher's message. For them Jesus' advice was to be applied to this life.

All of these facts make the modern squabbles of the churches concerning the differences between denominations seem surreal. It appears utterly pointless to be caught up in such debate when the fundamentals of their beliefs are being challenged so radically.

When uber-Catholic Mel Gibson's movie *The Passion of the Christ* was released it gathered criticism for its anti-Semitic tenor. This was emphatically denied by Gibson at the time. Looking at the film it is not difficult, however, to see where the criticism is coming from. The Jewish authorities responsible for crucifying Jesus come across as hateful, cowardly and highly malevolent. They even at times unfortunately appear as simplistic stereotypes. Those raised in the Christian tradition often hear of how Jesus came into conflict with the Jewish authorities, challenging them as hypocrites and followers of laws that have lost all meaning. They even receive the full blame for Jesus' death when Pilate washes his hands of his sentencing. 'The Jews crucified Our Lord' is a phrase that has still yet to die out. Given the bad press they get in the New Testament, particularly Matthews Gospel, it would have been difficult not to portray the Jewish authorities as the 'bad guys' in the film.

All of this is doubly ironic given what we know now about Jesus and his teachings. As mentioned earlier his message was almost entirely Jewish in nature but another point is that he probably only intended for Jews to listen and live by his teachings. There is no evidence that he ever intended for outsiders to become a part of it. The bad coverage given to Jews in Matthews Gospel is most definitely fraudulent and reflects a change in the Jewish political position when this Gospel was compiled, rather than Jesus' opposition.

Prior to it being written a bloody rebellion had been put down in Judaea that had reversed the Jewish position and made them deeply unpopular within the Roman Empire. Matthews Gospel would have been an attempt to distinguish this new following descending from Jesus' teachings from the older Jewish tradition by almost presenting Jesus as an enemy of the Jewish authorities. As far as its author's intent is concerned it was a major success. This complete refute of Judaism within the Gospels made Christians of the future view this ancient practise as existing only as a precursor to their own faith. This chauvinistic and patronising attitude would also be applied to many other faiths by future Christians. Someone once asked me if Jesus was Jewish. When I replied that he was they said it was a wonder that they didn't follow his teachings and convert. This is an indication of how it has become almost impossible by many to see Christianity for what it really is; Judaism for non-Jews. The description and image of Christianity being a Jewish splinter group is something many have shown difficulty in grasping.

Between Jesus' death and the writing of Matthew's Gospel the movement that traced itself to Jesus had moved from beyond Jewish confines to targeting the wider population within the Roman Empire. We know this to be almost entirely due to the vision and efforts of one man. After years of persecuting this new movement Saul would undergo a famed transformative experience on the road to Damascus. He believed he had seen into the true nature and meaning of Jesus' teachings and choose a new name in order to symbolise the change this experience had brought about in him.

Paul, as he was now known, used the teachings of Jesus to bridge the gap between Judaism and the wider population living under the rule of the Roman Empire. Where he disagreed with Jesus' other followers, such as Jesus' brother James, was whether non-Jews should be permitted to join the movement. It was this man, who had once persecuted the followers of Jesus, that is considered the closest we have to a first Christian. He helped develop the doctrine and teachings for this new movement in Europe by explaining various ideas in terms the pagans would understand and have been familiar with. Those pagans who desired to join the faith were known as God-fearers and amounted to considerable numbers throughout the empire. He placed Jesus, now considered the Christ (meaning an anointed one), at the centre of the movement because a human figure to represent the divine was more familiar and accessible than a purely transcendent God to the pagans.

The phrase 'Son of God' was a poetical Jewish description of a highly observant Jew. Being Jewish, when Paul referred to Jesus with this title he meant it completely in this sense. It is known that there were several different 'Sons of God' in the Jewish tradition, including the famous Rabbi Hillel. The subtleties of this phrase would often be lost on many of the pagan converts and their spiritual descendents.

Paul never believed that Jesus was the Son of God nor would have encouraged his followers to understand Jesus in such a way. The problem Paul would have found with this doctrine would be the thought of the transcendent God manifested and accessible only through Jesus and nothing else. The Judaism Paul would have been raised in would have found such a thing unthinkable.

Paul's efforts seemed to have paid of, in that converts became attracted to his version of Judaism. It dispensed with the numerous rules and difficult rituals, such as circumcision, that had put of many of the converts in the past. Paul had marketed his new version of

Judaism to the God-fearers well. The many letters he wrote to clarify doctrine and reassure these new converts would help shape the future direction the church would take. Paul's ideas of opening the movement to anybody would be the touches that would seal Christianities success. In such a class based and hierarchal institution like the Roman Empire this would have been a radical and even dangerous idea. In later times this vision of a universal (catholic) faith would make Christianity the religion of choice for an emperor afraid of his realm splintering.

Another phrase that has often been interpreted differently from its original meaning is that those spreading Jesus' message spoke 'with many tongues'. In years gone by many were told that this means they were able to speak in ways in which many others could understand them. Today it is better understood as a description of how the promulgators of Jesus' message lacked any kind of coherent or unified intellectual position or doctrine. This is not an uncommon occurrence in a newly formed movement. Orthodoxy requires an established tradition. What this phrase reveals to us is the number and variations of the followings tracing themselves back to Jesus. The Christianity that has come down to us through time is the only one of these variations to have survived.

The discovery of the Nag Hammandi texts in the Egyptian desert during the mid 20th century has helped us understand the nature of some of these other versions of Christianity. Among them are the Gospels of St. Thomas and Mary Magdalene. What they appear to be are Gnostic scriptures. The Gnostic practise was concerned with liberating the soul from bondage to the material world and into the realm of the purely spiritual to which it is seen to truly belong. In this kind of introverted religion the recorded events of Jesus' life were symbolic guidelines to an inner journey that ended in release from the corrupted world. Some have chosen to interpret these newly discovered Gospels literally with there references to Jesus and Magdalene's relationship. This would be a mistake since it appears most of the words placed in Jesus' mouth in these texts comes from older sources. Just like the writers of the four received Gospels, whoever compiled these texts was not concerned with literal truth but with the message these texts were to impart to the reader.

The Sword From The Scabbard

One of the most important Jesus descended traditions to remember were the Ebonite's. They are especially interesting because they were comprised of his original followers and so rejected all of St. Paul's initiatives. They emphasised only the originally Jewish nature of Jesus' mission and teachings. While Paul's version went on to unimagined levels of success the Ebonite's fell into obscurity. It is believed they were swept up in the rising tide of Islam hundreds of years later.

In its early stages Christianity was treated with distrust and suspicion by the authorities in the Roman Empire. They found its beliefs strange and disturbing compared with the various cults and followings of the day. The Romans had a live and let live attitude towards religion. This was a result of encountering the many diverse beliefs of the peoples they had conquered. Even if they had wanted to they had known, like most rulers will learn at some point, that this was an area it was best not to interfere with. Where Christianity didn't fit into this scheme of things was in its claim that its God was the only God and that faith in Christ was the only true salvation. Even the structure of its belief system was deemed irrational and strange.

Meaning in life was derived by the Romans and their peers through philosophy. Religion, for them, was not meant to explain why we were here. Instead, it was a series of rituals and practises that tied the practitioner in this life to the same rituals practised by their ancestors. It was a purely emotional experience that helped give those involved a sense of their place in the world. Even today this is what many experience religion to be. Many who go to Church do so because of the rituals that are played out before them and how it makes them feel. Punctuating each week with Mass or service helps give a sense of structure to their lives. Many of these people are uninterested in the history of their religion or the theology that surrounds it but recognise their faith as belonging to a realm completely separate from such concerns.

Another element the Romans found strange in Christianity that we often overlook today is the nature of its salvation. This is an issue which we rarely think of as being out of place if only because we are so used to it, but on analysis does raise serious questions about the nature of Christian salvation and belief. The issue can be raised acutely by asking what kind of a God brutally murders his own son because he is so in love with humanity? For the Romans it was this that made Christianity such a barbaric belief system.

Today crosses are often used to decorate homes without their owners really thinking about what they are designed to imitate. The crucifix is arguably one of the most hideous devices of execution ever devised. It guaranteed its victim the most drawn out and painful death imaginable. Many would argue that it is there only to give way to the resurrection but it is obvious that most of the Christian focus is on what is known as the Passion. The Stations of the Cross draw this process of pain and torture out so that each moment can be focused upon. Images of Jesus on the many crucifixes' that decorate homes often display the most horrific poses. Even the Christian slogan that Jesus died for 'your' sins makes it clear at what point in Jesus' life Christianity is most concerned with. Many other cultures and belief systems, since the Romans, have also found this focus on pain and suffering in a religion difficult to understand. For the Romans what was curious was the psychological condition of an adherent to this form of salvation. The perceived sacrifice of Jesus also went on to cause martyrdom to become a glorified condition among the early Christians enduring Roman persecution. Giving up their lives came to be seen as the ultimate act and test of faith.

Being treated like a strange and dangerous cult by the authorities caused Christianity to quickly take on a posture of adversity. An attitude arose within it of being a besieged but righteous island in a pagan and powerful world. This attitude would be rehashed and used again and again by Christians in the future. Even at times of strength cultures infused with this attitude would be quick to demonise enemies and see itself as being under constant attack by satanic forces as diverse as malevolent witchcraft or atheistic communism.

Despite these problems many still converted to Christianity even when it was made outright illegal across the Empire. Many of the reasons for this are obscure but it probably has a lot to do with Paul's idea for one religion for everybody. By opening access to anybody in a deeply hierarchal Empire it created an alternate spiritual Empire for people to be a part of. Here, slaves and rulers would be equal and able to mix outside of the social rules and norms that had limited them in the past.

Early Christians seem to have been sensitive to the criticism concerning the seemingly irrational nature of their belief system. The Greek philosophical discourse that their spiritual precursors the Jews had come to dislike found a new place inside Christianity. The Christian concept of God would find shaping and support in the ancient philosophy of Plato. His reasoning for an unmovable mover at the beginning of time and single source of all being would be used to rationalise the Christian belief concept of God. Although his arguments would not convince many today, at that time Greek philosophy and culture was quite widespread and popular in the Empire. That it could have been used to support the Christian cause would have pleased its converts and members. The adoption of Greek rationality also inadvertently lead to a highly anthropocentric view of the universe. The Judaic belief that God had created man in his own image was retained in the Christian tradition. This combined with the Greek concept of man as a uniquely rational creature formed in Christianity a highly human centred view of the universe. Most other cultures and traditions are different from this in that they place humanity firmly within and part of the world around us rather than having the world centred on us. This could go a long way in explaining our current sense of separation from the natural environment.

The final and longest lasting touches were placed on Christianity by St. Augustine. His writings would help determine what was to become the accepted orthodoxy in Christian belief. It would have been impossible for him to believe the extent his writings would influence the future. What he seems to have been mainly concerned with was the emergence of evil. Where had this force which encouraged men to sin originated from? Augustine's answer to this question altered the way in which Christians of the future would see themselves and their relationship to God. It is a doctrine that made Christianity seem even darker to non-Christians and remains controversial to this day. Augustine's explanation for why men and women are wicked towards one another is known as the Doctrine of Original Sin. By disobeying God in the Garden of Eden and eating from the Tree of Knowledge Adam and Eve had introduced sin into this world. This sinfulness passed through their ancestors into us today and manifested itself as human caused evil. Adam and Eve had suffered for their disobedience and made toil and endure hardship for the rest of their lives. This was now something all humanity was called upon to do to combat the Original Sin that they had been born with.

The most disturbing aspect of this theology is that it created an image of man as a permanently stained being. Due to the impossibility of removing Original Sin from their constitution there was no point in mankind trying to improve itself. Just as Adam and Eve had simply suffered and awaited judgement after being expelled from Eden man could only fear God and wait in hope. It was encouraged that people take part in good deeds but it was also recognised that these deeds had no effect on a persons chances of salvation. Such decisions were God's alone. We can see the effects of this kind of morality in the modern interpretation of ethics as a matter of choice rather than character. It is assumed we want to take the 'bad' path but sometimes manage to sum up the will power to choose the 'right' one. The idea of becoming a person who desires to choose the 'right' path is considered unrealistic.

Even today this form of theology strikes people as incredulous. What kind of God imposes such suffering on humanity because of a choice made in a mythical past? The image of a baby being born with inherent sin is also something many people find hard to comprehend.

Augustine's vision was deeply paradoxical in nature. It was gloomy and pessimistic but like Paul's, inclusive. Since all humanity was tainted by Original Sin all must suffer together on Earth. Happiness was not something to be reached in this life but to be hoped for in the next. This created a shift in emphasis from the present life to the next one. Whereas in the original Jewish interpretation the Fall was considered an essential part of a persons deliverance from immature beliefs in Christian theology it was lamented as a terrible mistake. The life affirming nature of Judaism was now lost from Christianity as a life of denial was held up as a paragon of virtue. This would have huge implications for the future development of Western civilization. Even the unconscious roots of today's War on Drugs can be found in this shift of emphasis. The kind of contentment and ecstasy felt during a drug induced experience was only supposed to be experienced in the next life. Touching upon it in this life was considered a form of blasphemy.

Other than their feelings on the importance of inclusiveness Paul and Augustine shared a similar concern with the issues of sexual relationships and women. Their unenlightened attitudes towards women would unfortunately also be adopted in large by the movement they helped shape. Augustine especially was disturbed by the sexual urges which he felt impeded his spiritual development. He famously called upon God to deliver him from such urges 'but not yet'. This difficulty with the issue of sex would almost become one of the staple characteristics of a Christian society. Within some sections of future Christian populations its very existence would go on to reach points of utter denial. Augustine's conclusion was that the Original Sin that infested human nature was spread from generation to generation through the act of sex. A flip side of this kind of repression and denial would become the level of sexual obsession endured by society today. This could even more accurately be understood as the previously repressed and private obsessions of some today made public.

In Roman society women were regarded with respect and often reached positions of great influence and power. There was a recognition here of what we know as hidden power. This concept when applied to women refers to their ability to influence events without appearing as heavy-handed or obvious as men. The divine feminine principle at work in the world was appreciated in fertility cults whose roots stretched back into prehistoric times. Even in later Christianity it would re-manifest itself in highly matriarchal cultures as the cult of the Virgin Mary that once incensed so many Protestant denominations.

Perhaps the contradictory and impossible image of a virgin mother being held up as an example of what women were intended by God to be also helped lead to this damaging attitude towards women. The frustration and shame attached to never being able to reach this level of purity because of sex could easily lead to painful inner conflict. The

The Sword From The Scabbard

Christian Trinity, which was comprised of two male elements and one androgynous one, also excluded the female element from divinity. Even the belief in the masculine nature of God is something that should be considered strange for an interpretation of divinity. It has long been recognised that Eve's encouraging of Adam to eat of the Tree of Knowledge has played a large part in this as well. For many it would come to appear that woman was responsible for introducing sin and suffering into the world. It would not take a huge leap of the imagination to see how sex itself became seen as the Original Sin responsible for humanities Fall. It is hard to gauge the full extent of the damage caused by this chain of thought. The widespread repression of sex has been seen to re-manifest itself as dangerous perversions and frustrations throughout history.

Even in today's world what appears to be one of political Islam's motivating factors is a hatred for and fear of emancipated women. Their strict and stunted interpretation of Islamic law forbids women the freedoms that are permitted them in the West. It is shocking that this seems to motivate acts of unbelievable cruelty and malice. One would- be bombers justification for targeting the London nightclub Ministry of Sound, was recorded as being that no one inside could claim to be innocent because of the way in which the 'sluts' attending dressed. The lead September 11th hijacker was discovered to have spent his last few nights alive in strip clubs. This is not only limited to Islam but through Christian history such frustrations and perversions are not difficult to find either.

In a more general consideration the hiding away of sex as a shameful act meant wide levels of ignorance regarding its details and proper practise. Many would find themselves in adulthood but still without any proper sexual education. It was also once not entirely uncommon in some parts of the world for marriages to take place due mainly to one partners desire to experience sex. Although today's obsession with sex, splattered across tabloids and music channels, has perhaps swung too far in the opposite direction, the Catholic Churches stance against contraception and premarital relations would be better understood as a conflict aimed at sex itself. It is also possible it could be another unconscious manifestation of the belief that extreme pleasure is not something to be experienced here on Earth.

In the year 325 the Roman Emperor Constantine was faced with an Empire politically and religiously diverse, even perhaps to the point of fracture. After securing his power base militarily he focused on uniting his subjects religiously. His was a new vision of an empire controlled not only in the material world but in the spiritual as well. For a people to be truly united he reasoned that they must share goals and views on the world and their place within it. Differences in this could lead to conflict and the disintegration of his realm. His idea's displayed many of the features modern leaders attempt to employ in order to justify policy. They try to unite the people they represent behind their causes and programs by making them appear to be always in those peoples interests. I doubt, though, if any of their attempts reach as far and have had such an impact as Constantine's. Tradition has it that he dreamt of a crucifix before battle and so displayed the cross on his soldiers armour. After winning the battle he took this as a blessing and message from God so converted the Empire to Christianity. It was around this time that the calendar was reconfigured to be dated from the birth of Christ rather than the foundation of Rome.

Constantine's choice of Christianity over the other religions under his rule probably has something to do with Paul's innovation of total inclusively. It is even perhaps this that gave him the idea of one religion for everybody. Most other religious followings under his rule would not have been seen as being open to anyone. Certainly not everyone would find Judaism easy to conform to with its emphasis on its own tribal history. Many of the other religions were too localised to be applied to the entire population. They relied on holy places and local knowledge of customs that most other regions of the Empire did not share. The Mystery Cults which were so popular at this time would have lost all point if the secret knowledge they claimed to grant to esteemed members was made public. Paul's unique vision had meant that his small Jewish splintering would grow to dominate Europe.

It has become increasingly clear, however, that to say that Constantine chose Christianity as the state religion is a flawed analysis. A more realistic view is to understand what was formed as a synthesis of various religious movements. All over the Empire pagan festivals would be converted into Christian ones and each region would retain its own distinct identity and version of Christianity. As history continued on even those elements of pagan practise that had died out re-emerged in Christian dressing. The huge plethora of Roman and pagan deities would return as the hundreds of saints available for people to pray to. The advantage of this was a figure to pray to for particular causes and needs. Just as pagans in a particular occupation prayed and looked to a particular god or goddess for guidance Christians would have a patron saint. If something is lost Saint Anthony will help you find it as the patron saint of lost things. The range of these causes is astonishing. St. Sebastian is the patron saint of Spanish policemen and chillingly, St. Judas is the patron saint of lost or hopeless causes. As mentioned earlier it is not difficult to see how places with particular emphasis on a goddess or fertility cult placed emphasis on the place of the Virgin Mother. A mother goddess would be reborn in this form to try and give balance to the highly patriarchal Christianity. Certain elements of the Mystery Cults would also be absorbed into Constantine's project. They also included stories of god-men such as Mithras, who had died and risen from the dead; a theme which appears to be common in religious traditions. The Catholic Church especially, is heavily indebted to the pagan elements absorbed into Christianity around this time, elements that were perceived to be shed by the Protestant churches during the Reformation over a thousand years later. Although many of them would claim to be seeking the original Christianity of the early Church fathers in many ways they could not be further apart.

Even in Constantine's time, as if foreshadowing this, various sects and factions within Christianity debated furiously over issues of doctrine. As a politician and military man Constantine had no time for the delicacies of this kind of debate. He ordered agreement between the various sides and eventually accepted what is now known as the Nicene Creed to be the official church doctrine. Many who repeat this creed weekly at Mass or service are unaware of the controversy or furious debate that came before its final endorsement. Even after that endorsement significant numbers disagreed with its final principles. These other sects only come to us today through archaeological evidence and historical testimony.

It was Constantine's decision to choose Christianity to be the main religion of his empire that sealed its global success. It would dominate Europe in this form for over a thousand years before splintering again during the Reformation and Enlightenment into a thousand interpretations and corruptions. Before then, however, it would spread with European culture to most corners of the globe where it has encountered great success today.

It must be wondered if Jesus, Paul or even Augustine ever imagined the extent of their decisions. No doubt they would find much to commend in what developed in their names. The highly anthropomorphic vision of God helped create a great respect for individuality and closeness to the divine. The acts of charity inspired by Jesus' teachings and focus on the feelings of love and compassion are points that cannot be argued with but only admired. These elements have gone far in shaping the goals Western society and people would come to see themselves pursuing. Aid concerts and the social justice campaigns that are a hallmark of modern popular culture have emerged from this impulse. There is much, however, that would not please them about where their teachings have led men and women. Even in regards to one another there is much in conflict. Paul took liberties with Jesus' teachings which he probably would not have recommended and Augustine's vision especially darkened Christian's view of the world around them. The Christian vision of Jesus as the literal Son of God became the pre-emptive fact of human life to those who believed. 'Our Lords' position and existence took the place of focus from the original teachings Jesus promulgated.

Today this can be seen in the self-righteousness of certain Christian groupings. Those who await the Second Coming and all others to be cast into hell do not display the forgiveness or compassion that is normally associated with Jesus' teachings. The arrogance and beliefs of superiority displayed by such sects would seem to be a primitive kind of revenge fantasy motivated by their lack of acceptance in the modern world. Although toleration and respect stretches from mainstream society towards these kinds of belief systems it is only because they are on the fringe and pose no real threat. It is difficult, however, not to be disturbed by the fact that among us walk individuals convinced that the rest of us are going to an eternal Hell when we die. In fact some would appear to relish this fantasy. As one astute scholar has noticed, Heaven would not be as much fun to these people or even worth going to if you did not get to watch others in Hell. Fringe groups like this seem to have existed in all traditions throughout history and in the world today. They seem to be able to take their own prejudice and hatreds and project them onto the divine realm. Reality is then shaped in terms of their own likes and dislikes. Their intense ongoing campaigns for converts betray the insecurities they hold with their own beliefs. The more people that believe something like this the easier it is to convince oneself that it is true.

Christianity, as mentioned earlier, is a hybrid of pagan and Jewish spirituality combined with certain elements of Greek rationalism. Its splintering in the past few centuries is not only into groups with fundamentalist leanings, such as those mentioned above but into other groups that would not even realise they were little more than corruptions of Christian church structure and beliefs. Most would believe themselves to be escaping or transcending all Christian influence only to display the worst elements of it. At least fundamentalism does hold some credence to Jesus' ethical teachings. Many of these regimes would reject morality and ethics in their entirety pursuing their goals.

To do this would have been made easier by the eccentric nature of Western Christianity. By distilling all conceptions of divinity into the person of Jesus all would fall if Jesus was doubted or proved to have not been divine. Christianities belief it was the only true faith encouraged a total psychological and metaphysical reliance on the divinity of Jesus. The existence of God, or divinity in general, became tied into this understanding of Jesus. Even Western ethics rested on this theological understanding of his position. Man was supposed to be good because God wanted us to be. We knew this through the teachings of his son Jesus. Therefore, If Jesus was proven to being merely human or belief that he was the Son of God was thrown into doubt it would create a kind of moral vacuum. By the 20th century this vacuum would come to be occupied in a number of different ways. The divinity of Jesus, a poetical description misinterpreted literally, became the cornerstone of Western meaning. The last few hundred years of Western history are an example of what happens when a civilizations pre-emptive fact of life is thrown into doubt.

The Sword From The Scabbard

2

NEW WORLD ORDERS

Tensions would always exist throughout the Christian era between what was seen as being truthful to its doctrine and the customs and beliefs which had preceded it. Even when the Christian scriptures were comprised from Greek into the Latin version that would mainly serve the Church until the Reformation, they were deliberately translated in a dry fashion to avoid the flourishes and decoration that were associated with classical pagan works. In various parts of the Empire tensions between religious authorities and local tradition would continue well through the first millennium. In many places compromise would have to be met between the official doctrine of Rome and other movements before it could consolidate power. Rival Christian traditions such as Celtic Christianity were often popular in their time but did not last as long as the better organised structures of the Roman church. With the eventual sacking of Rome and fall of the Roman Empire the church would still use its skeleton as a basis of organisation.

This conflict in Europe between the new Christian interpretation of the world and the classical knowledge and art forms now deemed heretical would seem to have mainly settled by the entry of the second Millennium. By this point even political leaders in Europe would seek recognition from the Pope, as the successor of St. Peter, for their legitimacy. Most of Europe was now united under one church as Paul and Augustine had once dreamt. The reintroduction of classical world ideas to challenge all of this would emerge from what today would seem like a highly unlikely source.

By the time the Renaissance occurred in Europe Islam had gone through several of its phenomenal growth spurts. North Africa and a huge stretch of Asia had converted too or were living under Islamic law. Unlike the slow growth of Christianity, Islam had practically popped up in less than a lifetime. In its golden age this tradition and its adherents would become one of the greatest civilizations in the world. It would stretch from Spain to Pakistan and hail some of the greatest spiritual thinkers in history. It was from here that the inspiration which motivated Europeans to move beyond their singular world view, resulting in the Renaissance, would emerge.

Most people have a grim picture of the Dark Ages that arose after the fall of the Roman Empire and before the advent of the second millennium. Renowned historians and thinkers have blamed this upon the rise of Christianity and its dislike of intellectualism or too much 'cleverness'. Recent historicism, however, quietly challenges this view. It would simply seem that the dispersed power structures that arose do not leave as much evidence or value historical records of themselves as much as more centralised cultures do. Saying that, however, it must be recognised that much of the rest of the world viewed Europe at this time as something of a primitive and barbaric place. It would also be fair to say that education and knowledge became limited to Christian understandings of the world. Who came to be considered the most educated and scholarly would be those in the clergy. Their access to the scriptures, written in a Latin most people would not have understood, stood them apart from the common man. The supernatural elements associated with these scriptures increased the perceptions of power they seemed to hold.

It is not surprising that the Renaissance took place in the city states of Italy. It was here that was the centre of the ancient world when it had surrounded the imperial centre of Rome. Its geographical proximity to the Islamic world also was instrumental in reintroducing the knowledge that had been lost in Europe.

As it spread out from its spiritual base in the Arabian Peninsula Islam never displayed the dislike of other forms of learning or knowledge that would characterise Christianity at this stage. Within Islamic culture the ancient texts and philosophy of Europe would be kept preserved to be rediscovered by their continent of origin. They included philosophical discourses of Ancient Greek philosophers, such as Aristotle, which were reintroduced to Europe in Arabic translations. This led to a growth of interest in ancient thought and artistic techniques that can be seen in the beautiful pieces created by the most famous artists of the Renaissance. The shift to more realistic depictions of people and environments this movement inspired shows us the increase in their interest in the world around them rather than quietly awaiting the next life.

These events led to huge changes in the nature of European thought. The 'pure' Christianity that preceded them would not return again in that form. Neither would the ancient philosophy now rediscovered from Muslim sources disappear. Eventually it would have to be amalgamated into Christianity by the man known as Saint Thomas Aquinas. His work meant Christianity was allowed to take on a more world friendly view of itself and he also benefited many lives in challenging Augustine's vision that humanity was supposed to only suffer on Earth. It was Aquinas' belief that God wanted humanity to be happy on Earth as well as in Heaven. This was taken into Christianity as a compromise between the re-emergent ancient thought and traditional church doctrine.

 The emergence of the Renaissance also provoked events to take a turn that could not be more different than Aquinas' vision of intellectual compromise. One of the visitors to northern Italy after it had been decorated in the luxurious Renaissance style was a man called Martin Luther. It was in part the beautiful artwork and the worldliness of the place that led him to seek reforms in the Church. He felt the true doctrines and teachings of Christianity had been lost in the pagan and worldly concerned nature of this place. There is a level of truth in his charges beyond just the aesthetically artistic nature of the churches and religious paintings. The Catholic Churches monopoly on belief and power had led to a certain amount of corruption within its structures. It became known for the clergy to charge members of their parish for services such as guaranteeing their place in Heaven in abuses of power that came to be known as indulgences. The other concerns Luther had over church decoration is even visible today in the decorative nature of Catholic churches and cathedrals while Protestant chapels and halls are much less embellished. Luther decided that some kind of reform would have to take place in order to deal with these issues.

Another major factor in the beginning of the Reformation was the invention of the printing press. Along with the Bible being translated into local languages this, for the first time, allowed the Bible to be made available to large numbers of people. This meant that the position of the clergy was placed under threat in that the common people could now approach scripture directly. Here is one of the sources of the Protestant dislike for the detailed clerical structures in Catholicism and for the primacy placed upon scripture within their traditions. Even today many Protestant denominations will not affirm any religious belief unless it has scriptural support.

Rather than being able to re-embrace its ancient past Europe travelled in a much darker direction. The forces unleashed by the Reformation and the counter-Reformation became obsessed with implementing their versions of the true nature of Christianity. Political opportunists jumped on board to take advantage of this division and consolidate their own power over their realms. The exclusivist beliefs, so puzzling to the Romans, of the early Christians now became the factor that tore Europe apart and turned it against itself. Since Christianity held it was the only religion that was true each denomination that splintered from the main church decried all of the other denominations as false. This is when Christianity took on an even more eccentric character in its obsession with doctrine and right beliefs that lasts until today. In an atmosphere electric with charges of heresy it was difficult, if not impossible, to approach new ways of viewing the world or exploring alternate versions of spirituality. This is one of the reasons Western Christianity never developed any kind of mystical or meditative tradition; something every other major world religion did. Any meaningful exploration of knowledge or development was stunted by the death sentence being available to those who deviated from the norm. Protestant denominations would have found a contemplative tradition utterly unbiblical and so not in the least bit Christian. The Catholic counter-Reformation would have found this individualistic approach to the divine close to how many Protestant churches viewed the individual's relationship through scripture with God and so heretical.

The Sword From The Scabbard

This growing obsession with belief systems rather than the actions of the believers, as in most other religions, can be best seen in how Christians would treat the discovery of foreign 'heathen' cultures. Debate abounded on whether or not the Native Americans possessed souls. It must have been confirmed because it was known that prior to slaughter thousands were baptised into the church in order to save them. The missionaries who accompanied the British Empire displayed this same understanding of religion. In their understanding only belief in Jesus Christ could ensure a souls salvation in Heaven, just as it was understood by the early Christians. No matter how an individual acted he would spend eternity in Hell if he did not accept Jesus as the Son of God. It is this that has helped motivate Christianity to spread itself through missionary movements further from home than any other religion.

The Reformation and its results has altered the way in which Westerners view religion in general. Many of us see the divisions between different religions being based on rival belief systems which contradict one another in the ways Christian denominations do, but the truth is more complicated. Many of the divisions between other religions are about different points of emphasis rather than different interpretations. Other religions are also much more concerned with our behaviour than our belief system, in other words being *orthroprox* rather than *orthodox*. Rabbi Hillel's Golden Rule was the words he recited when asked to repeat the huge Jewish Torah from memory.

The Reformation not only led to changes in the lives of Protestant believers but generally how the West would come to shape itself. The way in which the leaders of the Reformation stepped away from tradition entirely to implement change was something new. Today the West's attitude of non-conformity and exploring new realms of knowledge has the Reformation as its ancestor. Although the original Reformists saw themselves as harking back to the beliefs of the original Church fathers, eventually people would come to believe that their thoughts or actions did not need to have the backing of any past authority.

The shift in thought this led to was huge. Throughout history all civilizations and cultures have been deeply conservative. The traditions and customs of elders were seen to have been tried and tested and so found worthy. Ours has gone so far in the other direction as to almost institutionalise change. This helps explains why few of the beliefs that would have satisfied previous generations find the same acceptance in the world today. For example when asked why the Pope is the leader of the Catholic Church the given answer is that the line of apostilistic succession that goes back to Jesus' chief apostle Peter can be traced to the current Pope. This gives an answer that conforms to the sense of authority rooted in tradition that our ancestors lived by. As admirable as many of Pope's have been throughout history, (especially throughout the 20th century) in today's world that answer would convince few to believe that the Pope is God's representative on Earth. Instead we ask for something to be proven before we believe it. This is a relatively new form of thinking and has replaced tradition as the main method and source of authority.

The decades at the end of the 18th and opening of the 19th century are the ones in which the main stages of change took place that led us into the modern age. It was then that the principles of the Enlightenment would be applied to all areas of life and new conclusions would be reached that would shake the world and shatter long held beliefs. It had taken time but the method of trial and error we know as science had emerged, mainly because of its successful ability to predict and manipulate the environment, as a force to be reckoned with. Men, such as Isaac Newton, would show how the application of human rationality could be used to discover important truths about the world in which humanity had found itself.

The Enlightenment is considered by many to be the stage in which humanity managed to liberate itself from the darkness of the religious era and reached an age of true knowledge and reliability. Atheists especially count this era and all that resulted from it in high regard. Men like Newton and the other pioneers of modern science are viewed as almost saint-like by many in this line of thought. It is not difficult to see how a narrative like this can be constructed. The huge success of science and the power it seems to have given us over the natural world is hard to argue with. It often comes as a surprise to realise how eccentric its early proponents were. Newton spent a large portion of his time searching for a code he believed was hidden within the Bible somewhere. Just as many would after him, here he attempted to apply the methodology of reasoned and logical analysis to areas that were not comprised with the boundaries of rationality in mind.

The spread of literacy throughout these times meant that these discoveries being made about the natural world were not being kept to an elite but available to a significant portion of society. The methods of science also meant that anyone could perform the same tests and experiments for themselves. This all meant that huge changes were taking place in how people viewed the nature of knowledge. Rather than being tied to the authorities and customs of elders new information was being discovered about the world on a steady basis. Those in the Western world who were practising these methods came to see themselves as something entirely new. An image was formed of the entirely rational and autonomous individual whose relationship to nature was one of discovery.

The world came to be seen as being controlled by natural laws which were now open to human discovery. In many ways this was a deeply theistic image. For Newton these laws had been designed and put into effect by God, who then stepped away from his creation to watch it from above. Even when some people talk about God in the West today, this is often the image they have. It is usually always the conception of divinity atheists have in mind when they deny the existence of a God.

Newton's vision of God had set the stage perfectly for this kind of atheism. The Reformation had removed God from the world and placed him into the Holy Bible. Following this the Enlightenment had removed God from even the Bible and placed him outside the world entirely. Atheism was simply removing Him altogether. The interdependent nature of the laws that seemed to be governing reality did not appear to need an outside divine figure to put them into place. Often atheists imagine themselves to be heroic, rejecting the comforting illusions of an infantile humanity, in favour of a more realistic, harsher picture of the world. They see God and religion in general as a crutch for the weak which they have outgrown. The reality is that the way was paved for them by an inadequate and weak brand of religion which they are the logical conclusion of. God had already been banished to the edges of the cosmos before they took the not so huge leap of rejecting Him entirely.

It is here we can see how atheism was the result of the eccentric and strange direction Western Christianity had travelled in. Other religions encouraged people to regard God and divinity as a presence within their lives and the world around them. As mentioned earlier Judaism especially made an effort for people to feel the divine element of the world around them. For Muslims no part of life is beyond God's remit and for Hinduism God permeates and infuses everything. When encountered this conception of divinity is not as easy as a distant God to reject. The split between the religious and atheists today would seem to reflect this division. Atheists find it easy to reject the God in the clouds and resultantly scoff at what they perceive to be others belief in such childish and irrational things. Religious people, however, cannot dismiss the internal changes such belief has brought about and so remain undisturbed by atheistic attack. By separating humanity from God entirely Western Christianity had made it easy for God to be dismissed.

The rule orientated version of the universe conjured up by the Enlightenment has caused it to be routinely compared to a great clockwork. For Newton this clockwork had been wound up and allowed to run by God who then stepped away from it. For atheists it was entirely able to run by its own accord and so did not need direct interference from a supernatural power. Here and in many other ways this Newtonian universe made it impossible to reconcile received religious belief with new discoveries.

It is also this vision of the universe that created the modern conception of miracles. Instead of understanding the meaning behind the miracle stories or interpreting them in various ways they would now be understood in only one single and entirely erroneous fashion. The miracles would be viewed as Jesus defying the laws of physics, thereby proving himself to be the Son of God. This would also suit the scientific ethos of the era. As in all good scientific experiments we have a hypothesis backed up by evidence. As a result, today some await miracles and latch onto stories of such occurrences as proof of their faith. Most of us have met someone who tells us a story of some miraculous happening that defies the laws of science. They expect that science cannot explain it so it must be the work of a supernatural force such as God or perhaps Jesus working through one of the Saints. Waiting for a miracle before having faith, however, is a weak way in which to practise religion. Those who are religious based upon such stories and sightings are particularly susceptible to collapse of faith when faced with criticism. The kind of faith that is based on stories of miracles and such happenings is also very different from the kind of faith Jesus, as a Jew, would have encouraged. Again this a result of the unique nature of Western Christianity. Gone is the openness to divinity and quietude of true faith in all religions to be replaced by belief in doctrine supported by displays of happenings defying the perceived rules of science. Many cases of people today claiming to have faith have little more than a system of belief in certain metaphysical structures and historical events.

All of this is one example of how this new way of viewing the world would affect Christianity. This new way of thinking within rational and scientific boundaries meant that other forms of truth could not be perceived as valid. Unless the Gospels and biblical stories were literally true, for many they could not have any importance at all.

The later Romantic Movement was a reaction against this stringent and coldly logical way of thinking. Its proponents especially used poetry to display how truth can be revealed and passed on in differing and equally important ways. Their methods of describing the world and passing on experience would have been more akin to how those who wrote the gospels wanted people to read the texts. Those who read them literally, especially today, have been influenced almost entirely by Enlightenment principles. Religious fundamentalists would not understand or make this connection because of the generally anti-historical nature of their world view but in a large way the fundamentalist movements are highly modern ways of approaching religion and scripture.

In this way fundamentalists, atheists and even moderate Christians all share the Enlightenment belief that the only truth that really matters is literal truth. Other forms of expressing or sharing knowledge are deemed secondary, if important at all. Movements such as creation science are the offspring of such limited ways of thinking.

The Sword From The Scabbard

The other criteria for truth led down by the Enlightenment was that it must also be easily communicable. A scientific experiment can be repeated and if correct the same results will display themselves. Religious knowledge, as something private and often inexpressible, would have to change to conform to these rules. A religious experience would too easily come to be criticised as self-delusion or madness if it could not be explained or shared to a wider audience. The truth it held would be considered unverifiable and so invalid. Instead of focusing on the sense of faith within, this would cause Christianity to become increasingly externally orientated. Another influence it would have, especially within the Protestant traditions, was towards the individual's relationship to God. It was seen that all individuals should be able to talk to God directly and equally, without anyone or anything else intervening. Just as the practise and results of science could be explained to anyone it came to be reckoned that the practise and results of religion, such as being able to commune with God, should be open to anyone as well. The truth, however, is that such subjective developments and experiences will vary from person to person. Some believers will go their entire lives without any sense of the divine within it while others will experience it constantly. When all are encouraged to stay at the same level of talking to the divine it has the effect of stunting any exploration of other, deeper methods of trying to approach it.

As scientific exploration went on throughout the 19th century even more was uncovered which disturbed common understanding of the universe. Fossils were discovered of creatures no longer found on Earth. This seemed to suggest that God had allowed some of His creation to be wiped out. To understand how deeply shocking and challenging to the accepted world view this was it should be remembered that the first man to discover dinosaur bones concluded that they were placed in the Earth by God to test man's faith. People found it impossible to understand why God would create a species only to have it wiped out at a later stage. Not only did this contradict Biblical history, it also created an image of an uncaring and malicious God. The loving image of the Christian God was possibly the sorest loss endured by those Christians who lost their faith.

Other discoveries in geology backed up the old age of the fossils by revealing the Earth to be millions of years old. As another example of applying scientific standards to where they do not belong, some Biblical scholars could only date it back to 4004 BCE. Why, Christians wondered, would God create the world and let it sit for so long before humanity arrived?

The practise of historicism came to challenge the Biblical version of history and the Doctrine of the Incarnation. Attempts were made to historicise the Bible and make it less supernatural to avoid embarrassment by those who desired to still hold on to their beliefs. Such attempts were deeply misguided and resulted in dismal failure. Challenges to the Christian understanding of Jesus by historians armed with Enlightenment values and scientific methods proved to be, as seen earlier, especially damaging.

Even discoveries in astronomy changed the position of Earth in relation to the cosmos. The Church had tried to protect the image of an Earth centred universe from attack by different heretics throughout history. Now modern science had revealed the universe to be bigger than was ever imagined possible and Earth was most definitely not at the centre of it. Why was the universe so big if God had only created it for humanity to live in?

Except, as was becoming clearer to the men and women of the 19th century, He didn't. The Judaic and Greek influenced anthropocentric view of the cosmos had backfired, causing humanity to suddenly feel very small and unloved.

Amidst this concern over the increasing loneliness of humanity different scholars put forward ideas to reassure the public that God was still there and that he still cared for His creation. William Paley played his part in this by creating the famous image of the Watchmaker. When viewing the world Paley maintained that it's synchronised character and the advanced designs inherent within living beings was proof of a Creator. How could the world we perceive around us and the interdependent nature of the eco-system come together without some greater intelligent force to guide it? It would be as if coming across a perfectly designed watch set on the right time that had just happened to come together by itself. Such a thing could not be possible. As science revealed more about the detailed structures within living creatures and the increasingly interdependent nature of natural environments people found solace within this argument. Even today a similar stance is taken by those who espouse Intelligent Design. It was because of the popularity of this stand in the 19th century that made the discoveries and ideas of Charles Darwin so devastating.

Darwin was not the first to come up with a theory of evolution. Further back than two and a half thousand years ago the Ancient Greek philosopher Anaximander had proposed a similar idea. He guessed quite astutely that humanity may have developed from some kind of chemical or emerged originally from the sea. The reason Darwin's ideas were so controversial is because they explained away all that had been held up to support Paley's hypothesis. The amazingly complicated nature of life now had an explanation that did not require a supernatural force or higher intelligence. The reliance people had put upon the nature of life as a proof for God was blown entirely away.

Now the Earth was a speck floating in the universe and humanity was a by-product of an aimless and blind mechanism that relied on random mutation. Humanity was now staring into an empty void and trembled at what it saw. Instead of Gods beautiful creation the universe was a soul-less and empty machine. As more was discovered it seemed to reinforce this. The universe kept getting bigger, but in sickening lurches that reinforced humanities sense of smallness. The cosmos was beginning to look increasingly empty and without any discernable purpose.

This newly opened void, as explained before, was the result of the character of religion in Western Europe. It had collapsed under the pressure of the Enlightenment and would never be able to return to how it was previously. Its overemphasis on orthodox beliefs meant that when new understandings of how the world and life was created it was entirely displaced. This void was not only seen in the external world but deeply felt within. All values and meaning had been felt to be deeply tied to the Christian heritage and the world view it espoused. Without Jesus as the Son of God to tell us how God wishes us to live what was humanity supposed to do. The universe science was uncovering did not seem to give people any clue as to how to behave. Disturbingly, it was in fact, beginning to portray a world were the most ruthless would survive in an evolutionary struggle. The phrase 'survival of the fittest' was being increasingly used to articulate this understanding of life. It couldn't be any more further from Jesus' declaration that the 'meek' would inherit the Earth.

The ideas of Sigmund Freud would go on to deeply alter the way in which Westerners think. His methods of introspection and self interpretation makes people from the West today much more introverted and self questioning. Many of us spend as much time today in internal conversation as communicating with others. His science of Psychoanalysis dismissed God as a father figure for a humanity that was afraid to grow up. The uncovering of the unconscious mind also changed the way in which we view ourselves. To realise that we are motivated by unconscious forces within our minds and outside our immediate understanding makes us question every decision we make. When we stop and look into ourselves we are often surprised to discover motivations and desires there that we did not know existed and sometimes cannot even explain to others.

Living in a time when such ideas have been around for over a century it can be difficult to understand how deeply disturbing they were to Europeans of the 19th century. Not only was God being challenged but the entire way of life inspired by Christianity was being portrayed as a mistake. The values its adherents observed were actually beginning to seem entirely inimical to reality. Today less of the world is dominated by traditional Christianity so when modern believers feel challenged it is less of a blow. When most of Europe was faithfully Christian, however, it would have been deeply demoralising that the entire civilized world shared such a delusion. Some believed that a world without God and Christianity would mean humans would have to be more caring and loving towards one another, but without the metaphysical framework these ethics fitted into they lost all compulsion. Historical research and scientific discoveries had inadvertently come to rob the world of value and meaning. The projects to replace them, which would come to scar the face of the 20th century by making it the most bloody century in human history, would now be developed. All claimed to, but few ever really did, step outside of their Christian heritage.

The Sword From The Scabbard

These projects each attempted to forge a new place for humanity within the world. The most hideous and dangerous ones would claim backing from the scientific evidence and discoveries that had caused the intellectual collapse of Christianity. They would be shaped by Enlightenment principles, but in reality they were no more than corruptions and disguised versions of the Christianity that had preceded them. They allowed people to reconfigure elements of their religious heritage and outlook in what they believed were rationally acceptable terms. The displacement caused by scientific discovery would be cured by the sense of belonging these movements would bring to their members. The major problem with these projects, especially when in power, would be the easiness with which they could reject all ethics and moral accountability. Without a higher authority to be answerable to there probably would have been little struggle in doing so. It has also been noticed that many of those who decide to reject any form of ethics often suffer from the delusion that they are some kind of new being, differing from humans of the past. This delusion creates a sense of increased power and independence that would have helped motivate these causes. It should be noted that this is usually just as delusional as their belief in having become a new kind of human being.

The most important thing to remember about these attempts to give meaning to life was what colossal failures they were. Combined they are the most destructive developments in human history. It is impossible to get an accurate number of the lives which were lost or ruined by these earthly nightmares. The history of the 20th century now seems little more than a global conflict between these delusional followings and has been described aptly because of them as an Age of Hatred. Almost every nation in the world would adopt one of these programs at some point, often to the disadvantage of its own citizens. Reality would be rejected in a deeper way than ever before as ideological blankets would be placed over it.

The difference between these projects and political organisation previously was the extent to which they attempted to reach into the lives of ordinary people. In the past politics had been separated from the religious or metaphysical beliefs of the population. It had never attempted to give meaning to peoples lives in the way these undertakings would. In this sense they were more like religions than political movements.

There is a distinction made that applies perfectly in this case, between world-transcendent and world-immanent religions. These projects would be considered a perfect example of world-immanent religion. Their descriptions of and prescriptions for society included an explanation of humanities place and destiny within the world as well as a code of behaviour to live by. The way in which the leaders of these movements exploited humanities desire for meaning and the spiritual drive within them would seem to suggest that these movements certainly thought of themselves in such a way. They did not, however, refer to any element outside of the world or transcendent to perceived reality, as a world-transcendent religion, such as Christianity would. This could perhaps explain the reason for the size of their failure. They attempted to replace all religions but by rejecting the existence of any kind of transcendence or divinity left out the central element of one.

Within a religion non-believers were simply regarded as non-believers, heretics or infidels but in these systems of thought non-believers were generally considered an enemy which needed to be eradicated. Especially if that enemy existed within the regimes own borders. This, along with the rejection of divinely appointed ethics, could help explain the murderous nature of these schemes.

Communism covers a wide range of movements, from socialist orientated political parties whose Christian roots are easy to discern to the totalitarian regimes of the 20th century. The name most associated with the intellectual roots of this ideology was Karl Marx. He and Engels famously dismissed religion as the 'opiate of the masses'. For him Christianity tricked the oppressed classes into believing that they were to be rewarded for their faith and obedience in the next life. He may have had a point given the conditions of the industrialised world at this time and the level of exploitation and misery in most major European cities. He advocated revolution and the implementation of communism in order to cure these ills. What he had put together instead came to be an atheistic brand of Christianity.

The central crime that communism concerned itself with was inequality in society and the huge imbalance in wealth distribution that it was caused by it. The communist response to this was that all men were equal, a fact they hoped to reflect in a future communist society as all wealth would be shared equally and property owned in common. The idea that all men are equal has roots which are found in the Christian canon, such as Jesus' explanation of how all souls are equal in the eyes of God. Instead of a heaven in the next world, it would be in this life in the form of the future communist state. The main problem here is that any behaviour or action between now and the formation of this future heaven was permitted. Few ever imagined that the revolution would be non-violent. The apocalyptic beliefs inherent within Christianity can be seen here transplanted onto the future revolution. Instead of Jesus returning to augment an era of righteousness and justice the revolution would bring this about. Even the way in which Marx placed meaning upon history, as he split it into stages of human development that would lead to the communist society, betrays the Judaeo-Christian roots of his thinking. It is a peculiarity of Judaism and Christianity to place meaning upon historical events. To search the past for structure and developments in order to form a narrative which explains the direction humanity is travelling in is not found any other of the world's religious traditions.

For other traditions history is often seen to be illusory or deceptive rather than as exact as some historians portray it to be. We can see this today in which various historians constantly reinterpret the past with criteria from their own time influencing them. It is even easy to see how individuals reinterpret their own past to suit what they are thinking or how they are feeling on a particular day.

For millions communism replaced Christianity as the main hope of a better existence. The revolution would never occur in any of the industrialised cities Marx or Engels imagined it would. Instead bands of violent and aggressive groups would seize control in pre-industrial nations in the name of the proletariat (The communist term for the oppressed working class). Russia, China, Cambodia and other nations that had these systems forced upon them had never actually experienced the squalor of industrialised cities. The movements would gain the support of sections of the population who had a stake in the reversals it would bring to societal structures and left wingers from abroad. In the long run they would find that the best way to bring about control was 'through the barrel of a gun.' Often this would come along when the local populations began to realise the true nature of their new leaders.

The main cause of the brutal nature of these regimes would seem to be the method in which they came to power. The reliance of violence to gain control meant that those who can manipulate violent forces and use it to their gain would find themselves at the highest position of these movements. Shady characters such as Stalin, Mao and Pol Pot who previously would never have possibly come to such positions of power, found themselves suddenly in charge of millions of peoples destinies. These men, who would have probably become criminals if historical changes hadn't swept them up, were attracted to these movements because of the violence inherent within them. They found that the psychopathic behaviour which came to them so easily could be used here to their advantage. In any normal context much of the behaviour they would engage in would gain them a life sentence or worse.

The delusion of being able to wipe the slate of history clean and form a brand new society on rational principles can be traced easily to the Enlightenment. History has proven that this is impossible. Instead of making all men equal Russia would have Stalin as its new Tsar and China would endure Mao as its new Emperor. The dreams and political structures of these states were in many ways the same as those of the past but more concerned with regulating the populations thoughts.

The belief within communism that it was a condition of living that could be applied to all of humanity is often seen as Christian derived. The idea that all people can live under one set of beliefs is a hangover from the Christian belief that all people must be of the same faith in order to be saved. Now, instead of Christians, communists would see themselves as the harbingers of the one true faith. Even now many people still imagine a day when the entire world will be under one type of rule or government. Just as it was for the Christians and communists of the past this is a delusion.

The hero worship that became such a large part of these regimes was fuelled by the same devotional nature as found in religious belief. Now the leaders of the revolution would replace the saints and founders of the native population's religion as the figures of adulation and thankfulness. Stalin was to be admired for freeing his people from the fetters and exploitation of capitalism. Mao was to be worshipped for providing China with great events such as the Cultural Revolution and Great Leap Forward.

Atheism was also a large part of the communist conception of itself. Mao famously regarded religion as 'poison' and various groups were developed in Russia, such as the League of the Militant Godless, simply to mock and ridicule the churches. This was seen as an expression of communisms modernistic and scientific ethos.

Some people still see atheism as a highly modern and radical creed when in fact it is now an outdated and dying doctrine. What it has come to display most about its followers is a deep entrapment within a Christian world view. This is not just true in the case of communists but in atheists in the world today. By espousing atheism they do little more than define themselves within Christian structure by taking an intellectual position solely placed against some of its principles. As other ideas and ways of describing the world are being introduced to the West today they reveal atheism to be a highly limiting way to view the world. Today some imagine themselves to be free thinkers by adopting atheism, when they are doing little more than locking themselves into a Christian context.

It is estimated that between 1917 and 1959 the Soviet government, in pursuit of communist policies, had murdered 60 million of its own citizens. Before it collapsed it had come to dominate and occupy Eastern Europe without mercy. Many criticised or even lampooned Ronald Reagan's description of the Soviet Union as an 'empire of evil', yet the truth is that in many ways it was a most accurate title. The gulags hidden in the wastes of Siberia not only destroyed individual lives but spelt the destruction of the moral superiority communism claimed to hold over capitalist society. The support it received from abroad came from discontents ready to support anything other than the societies they were born into. Even if it meant supporting a totalitarian dictatorship with a homicidal leader. Today we can see the same trend in the way some left wingers have aligned themselves with right wing Islamists rather than their own governments or leaders. For some, so long as it is against there own government, it will do, no matter how morally repugnant it is.

Nationalism was another ideology that gained immense popularity in Europe through the 19th century. Ideas grew that races and nations shared spiritual bonds and common destinies. Each nation came to see itself as Gods chosen people in the same way as orthodox Judaism was perceived to. As the construct of the nation state was slowly put together it helped reinforce this sense of separation among the people of Europe. Each nation saw itself as the favoured one in conflict against the others. The phrase 'survival of the fittest' suited how many people viewed this struggle. Often nationalism was able to combine itself with other ideologies or religions of its time and so has managed to survive in weaker form until the present day. Anthems, football teams and days of national pride are remnants of this ideology, but few today pour themselves into it as was done in the past.

National heroes would be venerated in the same way communist leaders and Christian saints were. Men like Nelson or Bismarck would come to be revered as if in some way superhuman. Mythologies would be developed concerning the nation's history and struggles in the past. Often these stories would portray the nation to be constantly under threat from its neighbours and martyrdom would come to play a central and sinister role in this cult.

Eventually this state endorsed chauvinism would explode into the First World War. The sickly devotion to ones nation as an object of worship can be seen in the poetry from the early stages of war. The joy in which some seemed to be sacrificing themselves for their nation is reminiscent of the early Christian martyrs. Giving up ones life for ones people was seen as the greatest sacrifice and echoed the sacrifice made by Christ. The rise of nationalism in Western Europe had also combined itself with Darwinian science to come up with the conclusion that war was a good and admirable activity for nations to partake in. Darwin's discoveries were now being applied within humanity itself to create the horrible pseudo-science of Social Darwinism. It was right that only the fittest nation should survive, and the test of this would be open conflict. It often comes as a surprise to people today but the outbreak of the First World War was accompanied by celebration in every major European city. It was felt that at last the time had come for the people of each nation to prove themselves. As the war went on, however, the realities of such large scale conflict became more apparent and support for such blind nationalism waned. A great description for this war was once given as the collective suicide of Europe. Immortality for the generation that would be lost to this conflict was sought in the nation they hoped would last forever.

Writers such as Erich Remarque would capture the true cost of this way of thinking. He wrote perfectly of the utterly dehumanising effects that resulted from such naïve beliefs. As well as this, by being the first mechanised war it presented its participants with a whole new bunch of horrors, thereby ensuring that those who returned home from it were not necessarily survivors.

Later in the 20th century nationalism would linger on in a number of ways. Usually the independence campaigns of the imperial colonies would be influenced by nationalistic policies. In cases like Ireland it would be wrapped up deeply with the nation's sense of religious identity. The martyring of the hunger strikers in the War of Independence and the recent Troubles, along with their physical resemblances to images of Christ, would have struck deeply at the collective psyche of the Irish population. Gandhi's method of ahimsa, based as it is on Indian religious philosophy, would have formed a national pride amongst the population. Here they were fighting the British with methods developed entirely on their own soil rather than resorting to the violence the European powers had used to dominate the world. Gandhi knew that responding to the British occupation with violence meant slipping into categories they knew exactly how to respond to.

Although the borders between nations are slipping into insignificance today, nationalism will continue to exist as long as the nation state structure perseveres. At times of national threat it has shown a powerful ability to re-emerge. America's reaction to the Islamist attack in 2001 is a strong example of the solace and sense of security that can be obtained from zealous nationalism. In Europe, where nationalism has caused so much destruction in the past, people often dismiss American national pride as being little more than arrogance. It would appear that this dismissal is more likely born in part from jealousy in America's ability to be nationally proud without appearing racist or backward looking. In Western Europe, the birthplace of nationalism, extreme nationalist groups and thinkers have come to occupy the Far Right and are perceived negatively by the general public. It is probably for the best that this is so since they have based a large part of their platform upon racist, disguised as anti-immigration, policies.

Of all the ideologies that gave meaning to peoples lives after the weakening of Christianity fascism would become the most intellectually disturbing. Elements of it would create a new form of morality based upon early misinterpretations and misapplications of scientific discoveries. Fascism recognised the displacement and alienation that resulted from the Enlightenment and the industrialisation of the 19th century. As mentioned before the radical changes implemented meant that people had lost their sense of place in the world. The old feudal systems of Europe that had categorised people into their class and gave them an idea of how to live their lives had fragmented as well. For fascism this was to be cured by giving the people a place within a new system. The central distinction of fascists was that there must be someone strong to give this to the people.

Fascism's heyday was between the two World Wars and while an economic Depression was sweeping the world. In the nations where it took hold daily conditions had become intolerable for the population. Many found communism suspicious or undesirable and now, because of the Depression, it appeared that capitalism had failed as well. The answer to all of these problems was seen as the need for a strong and able leader. Democracy was being increasingly seen as a weak and factional form of government. A dictator would have to be allowed to control the nation, for the nations own good. While communism planned for itself to conquer the globe, fascism was highly localised in nature. Nationalism would come to play a large part in its world view, albeit in an exclusively racial form.

The Sword From The Scabbard

Fascisms most famous and extreme stand was in the National Socialism of Germany. The theories of the Social Darwinists not only inspired the Nazis but influenced their behaviour. Some of their lead thinkers came to believe that they could manipulate and direct evolution in order to create a better future. This idea was not a distinctly German one however. In several American states sterilisation of the handicapped and insane had become law. These misguided goals and the simplistic thinking behind them would eventually culminate in the 20th centuries defining event; the mechanised slaughter of European Jewry in the Holocaust.

The precursor of the authoritarian nature of fascism can be found in the structures of the Catholic Church. The way in which its officials touched upon every aspect of life was reminiscent of the relationship between Catholic clergy and the lay population. It should be noted, however, that throughout its existence Nazism was deeply opposed by the said Church. It is now known that Pope Pius XII was prepared at one point to help plot the overthrow of Hitler. This does not mean, however, that Nazism was not influenced by the structures and authoritarian atmosphere Catholicism was able to develop over its flock. Dermot Morgan, in the popular series *Father Ted*, joked about these similarities when he said 'fascists dress in black and tell people what to do, priests….'

As in nationalism, the mantle of being the chosen people was taken from the Jewish race and placed like a crown upon the German head. Their racial theories held up a new history of humanity based upon racial history and struggle. There was a hierarchy within humanity with the Aryan race at the pinnacle, being represented in the modern world by the Germans. Other races such as the Slavs, Jews and Negros were now automatically considered inferior. Even normal Darwinian science was hijacked to back the Nazi's conception of the world. The perceived brutality and harshness of evolution was jumped upon as an excuse for cruelty and barbarism. Destroying the weak, infirm and those judged unworthy could now be excused as protecting the future of humanity. Compassion and normal human values were dismissed as a stronger morality was to be formed that would not allow itself to be sucked down by such sapping feelings. As the new chosen people Germany would need a new messiah; someone strong and powerful who would lead them into a new era of freedom and glory. A place was created for a man like Hitler to step into and fulfil his nation's fantasies. Lifted now to the pinnacle of power, this man would project his own insecurities and complexes onto a global scale, destroying the lives of millions in the process. The devotion that was held in fascist nations towards their leaders is difficult for people in today's western democracies to fathom. This is in part because the modern dislike and distrust of politicians and political leaders derives from the totalitarian trauma of the Second World War. Never before was it revealed to the world how far people could go to follow one mans blood soaked dreams.

This trauma can also be seen in the way the far Left in the modern world are ready to oppose any form of authority without being able to advocate any kind of workable alternative. The attitude that all forms of authority are automatically perceived as a form of oppression has led to a culture of deviance disguised as dissension. It has almost become a cliché in movies and other forms of fiction to have a totalitarian government as the enemy. Every act each government takes part in to increase its own people's security is used in dystopian fiction and conspiracy theories as the next steps towards dictatorship. It is this Second World War trauma that allows some of those on the extreme Left to even produce documentary movies attacking their own government during a time of war.

Fascism deliberately bypassed the intellect and aimed itself at the human centre that was normally reserved for religion. Its immense rallies and colourful symbolism touched upon the emotional core of its adherents. While communism made great attempts to explain itself intellectually, Nazism made no such endeavour. It has in fact been recognised that Nazism had a kind of deliberately anti-intellectual character. It saw the arguing of thinkers and highbrows as a divisional waste of time. What was needed was action and unity. By transcending the intellect it provoked experiences and emotions among its followers that tied them to the movement at the deepest level. A background mythology of racial superiority and an expected purification of the future brought about by a messiah figure cemented Nazism as a truly world-immanent religion.

The Sword From The Scabbard

Fascism perished with the end of World War Two, persisting or popping up as smaller dictatorships in places like Spain and Iraq. Communism held on as a viable threat until collapsing with the Soviet Union in the late '80's and early '90's. It was because of this that around this time some political commentators predicted a kind of 'end of history'. Extreme nationalism had exhausted itself, communism had failed and fascism had been defeated. The political system to emerge out of this and be declared by some as victor was liberalism. Combined with a democratic government it has been quite rightly described as the 'least worst form of government yet'.

Liberalisms central concern is with the individual. The word used by those loyal to it and to help justify its spread is freedom. Today's war in Iraq began as an attempt to impose this kind of freedom upon the Iraqi population. It is not impossible for this to happen, but something many of those attempting to impose it on Iraq need to recognise is its Christian roots. Jesus' teachings were aimed at individuals and their private ethical considerations. He taught people to be respectful, tolerant, reasonable and to care for one another. This cherishment of the person by others manifests itself as liberalisms emphasis upon the individual as the central focus and building block of society. The Christian belief in the eternal soul plays its part here as well. The idea that deep inside us there is element that makes us all unique and separate has evolved here into the belief of people as autonomous units. Even the Western concept of personality has its roots in this doctrine.

Liberalism first developed strongly in Protestant nations such as Britain and America because of Protestantism's emphasis on the individual conscience. Dislike of authoritarianism and centralised power stems from the distrust and suspicion that was previously held towards the Catholic Church. Unlike Nazism and communism where individuals were parts of the whole, liberalism has the whole existing only to serve the individual. This helps explain why liberalism has been the main ideological enemy to both these creeds.

Liberalisms survival may be down to its adaptability. Late 19th century liberalism enabled the richest members of society to hold on to their fortunes. It held back the government from imposing laws that would restrict business by increasing taxes or writing new labour laws. Freedom for the individual here meant freedom from government interference. Modern liberals desire freedom for the individual as well, but calls upon the government to interfere in their interests. Big business is considered modern liberalisms enemy and it calls upon the government to help contain it. Today, when it comes to economic policy, those who call themselves conservative or right wingers are the same as 19th century liberals. It is an indication of how far liberalism has gone in conquering Western nations that even those who distance themselves from liberal policies are heavily influenced by older liberal policies.

Individuals are protected in liberal nations by a system of law and order that attempts to protect each of us from harm, whether from one another or from the government. In most liberal societies that is joined with a democratic government, which gives each individual a say in how the government is run. The government normally is divided in order to prevent the accumulation of too much power which is seen as the precursor to the liberal evils of totalitarianism and dictatorship.

Enemies of liberalism have always portrayed it as giving rise to a weak and spoilt population. Decadence is normally the term applied by these regimes and followings to it. By catering to the individual and what he or she wants in life it is seen as creating a population unwilling and unable to fight. Communists saw it as the bastion of evil capitalism and that it was only a matter of time before it would collapse as such. The Nazi's thought that liberal societies were fractured and lacked any kind of strong leadership. They also thought they would not be as willing to fight and so not as capable when it came to war. Although the first part of this belief can in part be true the Nazi's found they were wrong on the second half. Modern Islamists, the heirs to fascism, have similar beliefs regarding the liberal West. It is decadent and loves life so much that it will be afraid to fight. Like the Nazi's they will find they are mistaken. The good condition of life in the West makes its members willing to fight to preserve it. It is true that liberalism, because of its life affirming nature, abhors war. It is to be used as a last resort and usually in order to protect citizens or the interests of citizens from harm. Even the highly dubious war in Iraq had to be justified to the public as an attack on a fascist dictator. The fact that it has been so unpopular in the West because many perceive it to be motivated by selfish interests indicates the depth liberal attitudes to war have permeated society. Even in times of war violence is permitted for military advancement only. When stories leak in Western media about it being used arbitrarily or in prison systems the reaction is of revulsion. This differs significantly to the Islamist use of terrorism and its goal of as much death and destruction as possible. Or Hitler's twisted need for a perpetual war to help strengthen the will of the people.

Liberalisms greatest strength, however, is the diversity encouraged by the freedoms it grants individuals. Within a liberal and open nation all cultures and traditions have the potential to co-exist. Liberalisms dislike of coercion, bigotry and centralised power along with its values of toleration, co-operation and respect allow different belief systems and ways of life to flourish. In this sense liberalism can be considered a meta-ideology, since it allows other methods of thought and life to exist within it. The freedom that protected the economic market for 19th century liberals is now used to protect the rights and beliefs of individuals. This creates a diversified population that has proven to be highly beneficial to any nation that fosters it. New ideas and ways of thinking prevent a culture or nation from becoming stagnant or left behind in today's world. Countries that value their economies have deliberately encouraged immigration and diversification. It is even a feature of liberal democracies to allow those opposed to liberal values to have their say without discrimination or bias. Racist political parties, fascist groupings and communist movements have all been tolerated today and in the past. Even in some cases they have been permitted to run for election. The benefit of living in a free society is that movements like these can be seen for the bad ideas they really are.

One of the elements of liberal society that is often cited is religious freedom. Unlike communism and Nazism, liberalism encourages the individual to practise religion freely and without interference. The government is normally, or at least nominally, secular and so does not interfere with the beliefs of its population. This has developed in part as compensation for the religious wars that once tore Europe apart. It should also be recognised that secularisation is a concept that developed from Christianity also. The idea would not have been possible if Jesus had not advised to give 'Caesar what is Caesars'.

While liberalism developed in the 19th century science and atheism were on the rise, so to run a nation on religious lines would have seemed ridiculous. It would have been felt by some, just as in communist nations or scientific circles, that it was only a matter of time before it disappeared altogether. In the meantime it would be tolerated so long as it didn't influence governmental or economic policy. Modern liberals dislike the idea of religion influencing politics at all. Often the negative aspects of Christianity are what they have in mind when they think of it. George W. Bush's religious beliefs are considered by them to be a deep liability. Across the Atlantic in the most secular region of the world, Western European governments are careful not to appear religiously orientated at all. The secular ethos, rather than a stance of neutrality, has come to be seen as an integral and positive element of liberal society. Any kind of governmental religious bias is seen as contrary to the pluralistic society liberalism is supposed to foster.

For many in the West what has developed today is the final answer to the political developments of the past few hundred years. Religion has been discredited along with communism, fascism, nationalism and any other attempted system of political control. A liberal democracy with a dependable legal system and the free market to provide the populations needs has proved to definitely be the least worst form of government. Even after the collapse of the Berlin Wall ideology itself has become suspect and a more pragmatic method of governing has been advocated. This has proven difficult to accomplish. Although few challenge the perimeters of liberalism ideologues still rise to try and influence government. Today's come in the form of free market fundamentalists and libertarian neoconservatives. As well as this those who count themselves as being on the ideological Left within these nations have yet to offer any kind of realistic alternative whatsoever. In America they spend their time making movies and in Britain they seem to have died some time in and around the 1980's. There are plenty of works sitting on bookshelves which criticise the current governments and their policies but few which suggest anything constructive. The far Right has been portrayed by the media, not entirely wrongly, as being the political representatives of evil. The type of government in most Western nations today has proved the most effective for providing their populations with their material needs and keeping them safe. At the end of the day this covers a lot of the area that should be expected from a government and much more than some of the alternatives offered. It is right that the fantasies of a political system ushering in a golden age are being completely dispensed with. The only political faction operating today that still seems to be really fighting for this kind of fantasy is the modern fascism of political Islam. It can be only hoped that true Muslims, in the future, are able to extinguish this base and superficial version of their faith.

Today the world's most powerful nation's brand of liberal democracy and economic policies are being emulated, along with its culture, across the Western world. The ideological struggles of the last two hundred years could also be understood as the gradual rise and acceptance of American values and political structures. Often this is seen a being aided, if not caused by, globalisation.

The rise of anti-Americanism is something that should be expected when a nation becomes as powerful as America has. Those powers and nations who wish for themselves to be in this position complain and criticise every action America takes part in. American behaviour during the Cold War is often portrayed as ruthless and aggressive, as if the enemy was in some way an innocent victim. Intervention in the Albanian crisis during the 1990's to prevent genocide, was actually criticised as a war mongering media ploy. The Second World War trauma that causes all forms of authority and power to be despised by many left wingers plays its role here also. In the European nations that once were the centres of world power anti-Americanism is especially fervent. In recent years this has reached levels that are difficult to understand. Many Europeans claim to sympathise with the insurgents in Iraq or even admire Putin in Russia for standing up to America. Even in one case when I heard someone say that they prefer that America won the Cold War to the Soviet Union I heard someone else challenge him by asking what he thought was wrong with the Soviet Union. The real question being what this individual thought was right about it. Perhaps, in a weak form, the salvation through politics dream is still alive among anti-Americans in Europe. This salvation has nothing positive to describe or offer, but only the escape from American power.

For medium sized powers such as Britain and France American power is something to envy. The security blanket that America has thrown down over the world is something that prevents these powers from gaining the strength they once held ever again. This can be seen in that the criticisms from people in these nations towards America would be better suited to their own nations past behaviour. Smaller nations have everything to gain from this security blanket, especially since it protects them from the medium sized nations.

America does not like to think of itself as being imperialistic, but the fact is that it does hold a power over the rest of the world that no emperor of the past would have dreamed of. It is an empire, however, that differs greatly from those in the past and probably wouldn't suit the despots who controlled them. America seems to take to its position with a degree of reluctance, preferring other nations and peoples to take care of themselves. The principles built into its foundation documents and the values that it counts as American prevent it from condoning harsh or dictatorial rule. The deeply religious character of the nation has also played its role in shaping the values and principles America tries to import. Modern culture around the world has been shaped by America, not because it has been forced to but because it has found itself popular. People have found the American model attractive because it offers chances and opportunity no other system can. Its politically enshrined values are attractive because they correspond to what most cultures consider to be morally right. The recent excesses of the Bush regime that has attracted so much hatred and resentment will come to be seen as an aberration born of 9/11 trauma. Already Americans seem to be reinforcing the values their nation is celebrated for. In the running for presidential nominations the

The Sword From The Scabbard

Democrats have put forward Barak Obama and Hilary Clinton to challenge the white male domination of world power.

The values that have been adopted from America and promoted throughout the worlds liberal democracies are now so entrenched that we barely realise there was ever something different on offer. The individuality liberalism respects is especially prominent in the American system. There are a wide range of factors, including historical, economic and religious ones that have caused this. What it has led to in modern society is what is known as the cult of the individual. All around us this cult is promoted through the media and manifests in how we regard ourselves and our interests. Being a real individual often appears in many cases as the ultimate goal in peoples lives. We are all encouraged by movies and television to be ourselves and not to conform to any outside pressures. What this has led to is a quest among large numbers of people to find themselves. Social networking websites such as MySpace and Facebook may feel natural to take part in but they would never have been possible but for the highly individualistic ethos and deep belief in the personality that has developed in the West.

Within liberal democracies the 20th century's obsession with politics has been relinquished in exchange for people 'following their dreams'. In a way this lack of interest in politics is probably the signs of a healthy system of governance. So long as things are comfortable for the population they will probably not be overly concerned with politics. While some conspiracy theories portray this as the government tricking its population into conformity with its rule, it is more likely an acceptance of adequate governance. Only when something is threatening or dangerous does a rise in political interest seem to occur.

One of the most interesting and important parts of the American model to be emulated is what is known as the 'pursuit of happiness'. It is likely that this contributes heavily towards the success of liberal democratic model. It recognises a want deep in the heart of humanity and builds a political system that not only respects this drive, but intends for itself to further it. Individuals are allowed and expected to seek out and find whatever it is that makes them happy in the world. With Christianity appearing discredited and chances of eternal bliss in the next life considered slim this has caused modern Western society to become deeply life orientated. Modern society attempts, or at least claims to give, individuals the opportunity to find happiness in this life by allowing the possibility of people to fulfil their individual dreams. What that dream of happiness was to be based on is considered up to the individual themselves. Of course the Western democracies have not always lived up to this ideal and certain opinions of what happiness is have come to predominate over all other options.

Today world-transcendent Christianity takes one of two forms. It is either in the background to normal life as a kind of social obligation but not interfering in the individual's private pursuits or else dominating life in its fundamentalist form. The first version is a hollow and empty example of what a religion is supposed to be while the second is impossible to accept without lying to ourselves. The political and ideological projects which ended in complete failure could be considered world-immanent versions of Christianity. It would even appear that there are elements built into their very nature that caused them to collapse. Yet liberalism, with its own Christian roots, has not fallen or been discredited in the same way.

This can be understood in that liberalism can be counted somewhat different from most of the other projects since it does not intend to create some future utopia or have any apocalyptic fantasies. Even if some people did have such dreams they have been laid to rest in the killing grounds of Iraq. Its development has been slow so the quick regime changes and massive upheavals associated with other ideologies have never been a feature of it. Another advantage is that it has developed to the needs of the people rather than developing something inhuman that the people need to be used to serve. So long as it appears to not interfere unreasonably with the population's pursuit of what it wants its values and ideals will remain successful. Meanwhile as the people within this system we are free to pursue self-fulfilment and our interpretation of the good life without interference. The mantra and oft repeated advice of today is to do whatever makes you happy and here is where the propelling force and sustaining strength of modern society derives from. It has recognised a burning human drive that it promises to help foster and fulfil. Where most of our social problems today have risen from is the limiting of the definition of happiness to something utterly shallow and unfulfilling.

PART TWO

The Sword From The Scabbard

.

3

Left Wanting

The previous chapter ended with the establishment and acceptance of the liberal democratic model throughout most of the West. With this values such as freedom, human rights and equal opportunity and treatment have become unquestionable features of modern society. Generally people have realised the size of the ideological failures and revolutionary politics no longer has any support meaning that most of today's issues and debates are all contained firmly within the system. People have looked elsewhere for the hope and support that was once gained from dreams of a future perfect state.

The suffering and difficulties that are encountered in life were once justified in that they gave way to a heavenly bliss. When this fell through pain and misery were justified in that it would lead to a future unflawed society on Earth. It is not only the escape from or justification for the suffering and pain in life that people sought but the actual acquisition of happiness. When enough people were convinced both of these goals were accessible through political means the ideological projects found the fuel they needed. To escape the wretchedness and shame of being poor become a communist and help build a state in which all will be equal. When Germany suffered defeat in the First World War redemption was to be found in reasserting itself and re-fighting the war.

The Sword From The Scabbard

These are the kinds of ideas that not only offered escape from the pain of the present but once gave people the feeling of and hope for lasting happiness. Today we recognise theses dreams as dangerous delusions that increased the world's misery rather than curing it. Modern society no longer makes such claims for itself. Instead it is designed to step back and allow people to define and search for that kind of happiness or contentment themselves. When it is expected to step forward is when some person or people are disadvantaged unfairly and need assistance. In this sense it provides the welfare state and the forces of law and order. The state does not dictate what kind of life someone should lead and provided they can maintain themselves and do not impinge wrongly on others attempts to live life they are left alone.

As for their goal and drive in life it is entirely up to them. This allows for a diversified and pluralistic society to form along with the free association of ideas that comes with it. Combined with a free market individuals from any background can try to become successful in order to change their economic and social conditions, if they wish to do so. Success can never be guaranteed but is always possible. Free debate and open discussion allows for good ideas to be identified and bad ones dismissed. This can mean all the difference in whether a society survives or not.

The main strength of modern liberal democracies has also turned out to be the main cause of the worst problems within it. Societies in the past had their members born with meaning in their lives. Being born in an entirely Christian society meant being born to worship and serve God. Meaning in life was never even considered an issue open to debate. It was clear as handed down through tradition. This meaning began to be questioned and challenged with the Enlightenment so people found a more believable meaning for their lives in the ideological projects. Now in a communist society life was lived to help bring about a perfect world. An important element in these cases is that of compulsion. People felt compelled to worship God because hell fire awaited those who did not. Communism had to be brought about or people would suffer under capitalist rule or others born beneath established communist rule were compelled to adhere or risk their personal safety. By not compelling people to live any particular kind of life, within liberal democracies meaning in life has become an issue for those born in them. Since no way of life seems important enough to compel people to live it, many born in these societies have felt that this is a true reflection of reality, and so have lost the ability to believe life may have some granted meaning. There is no doubt that not having compulsion of belief in society is one of its most favourable features but this does not mean that it doesn't have any negative effects.

We can see this phenomenon at work in that many have latched on to some of the liberal democratic features, designed only to assist in life, for meaning in it. The free market is designed to provide food and products to make life possible but has been used by many as a new centre of life. Fantasies of being rich and successful have even overtaken the dreams of those who look forward to a heaven. The entire drive in many people's lives is concerned entirely with money and the status inherent within it. For others the cult of the individual has taken centre stage in providing meaning to life. The desperate search for fame that runs television shows such as Big Brother and The X-Factor is motivated by this obsession. It would seem that for many this is the closest to immortality as it is possible to get. Another trend that has been caused by this cult has been the growing self-preoccupation of individual members of society. Social networking sites display the amount of time and thought modern people put into shaping their identities and defining themselves in ways they would like others to see. In more recent times this has almost grown into an obsession, as can be seen by the proliferation of lifestyle products and magazines. These are small and shallow activities used to distract a drive that once provided great meaning and contentment to life. The redirection of it into small and ultimately empty things can lead only to long term frustration and sore disappointment.

An essential element to understanding these activities of today and the past is in the promises that are laid down by them. The goal of the Christian life was to reach heaven where the soul would endure a bliss that was beyond earthly comprehension. The future communist society was designed to cure all economic ills, thereby curing all of the world's problems since according to Marx they were derived from economic factors.

The Sword From The Scabbard

The modern desire for richness is understood as opening up the means for and securing a better present and future. Fame and recognition is seen as the crowning moment of the cult of the individual and the ultimate escape from obscurity. Other modern drives such as the search for a loved one, glorified by television and cinema, means escape from the highly atomised nature of society and the full acceptance of oneself by another. What each of these claims to offer its believer is escape from their sufferings and the attainment of a real and lasting contentment and happiness. Salvation, in whatever form it takes, promises an end to personal suffering and conflict.

It is this search for a level of contentment that consciously or unconsciously appears to be the main motivating factor in human life. It can be said with some confidence that humanity are happiness seeking creatures. One of the most harrowing recorded aspects of chronic depression is how its sufferers are convinced that not only is happiness unavailable at the moment, but it is impossible to ever attain. It is also noticeable, in people who do not suffer from this condition, how despair arises when they feel happiness is out of reach for them. In our society this willing and desire for happiness is deeply taken advantage of whether we know it or not.

Sigmund Freud's work on human nature and psychotherapy has already been mentioned as deeply influential on how Westerners view themselves. Where it has also come to shape our lives is through the medium of advertising. In today's world advertising is considered of the up most importance. It is considered essential to keep people aware and informed of the various products available through the market. All over the media and throughout towns and cities we are constantly being bombarded by reminders of various products that are now available to help improve our lives. Within the free market interpretation of the world we have all taken on the sole role of consumers. It is this part that we play that has come to help keep the entire market healthy. It has become almost essential for people to keep spending money and buying things in order to keep their nations stability intact.

This situation humanity has found itself in is rooted in the work of Edward Bernays, the nephew of Sigmund Freud. It was his uncle's work on human psychology that inspired

The Sword From The Scabbard

Bernays to change the way advertising was developed in America. By revealing humanity to be motivated overwhelmingly by unconscious drives from deep within Freud challenged the belief that a human being could make decisions on an entirely rational basis. Bernays changed advertising by not appealing to persons rational needs but to their deep seated emotional drives. Now humanity would become constant consumers as buying products no longer was only concerned with the needs of the population but their wants. Advertising would use the truths discovered by Freud to constantly invent new wants for the population. Wants that would sometimes even be disguised as new needs. How this was done was by having the advertisements display people using the products being sold and appearing to be content and happy because of it. This seems to be simple and basic advertising principles to us today only because we are so used to them. What we forget is just how successful this simple ploy really is. Companies have now made billions through their advertising agencies fostering the appearance of selling happiness.

If all of this sounds sinister or malevolent it is mainly because it mostly is. When consumerism was first invented in the 1920's it was out of the fear of Marxist economic ideas spreading. People had to be convinced to keep spending money and believing in capitalism. What was to drive this system forward if people found satisfaction in what they owned and slowed down their consumption rates? A system had to be developed that would prevent people from becoming satisfied and buying only what they needed. It aimed at convincing people they were not spending money on their needs but on their deepest desires. This has proved so successful that modern day economics is entirely dependent on a system that constantly promises happiness and contentment but makes it almost impossible to attain.

The deep seated want of happiness in human beings also helps explain the high levels of drug use in the West today. Those born into highly consumerist societies often become tired and disillusioned with the promises advertising makes. The enjoyment of goods and property is fleeting and weak compared to the enjoyment that many have gained from the use of recreational drugs. Some individuals are actually confused by the popularity of drugs among considerable numbers of people today given all of what is now available and open to them in the modern age. It does not seem to occur to them that the advantage of spending money on mind altering substances is that there is more of a chance of enjoying the experience than spending money on goods or on trying to make more money.

The situation of constantly promising but not delivering happiness coupled with the modern lack of meaning in life has provided fertile ground for depression and other related emotional difficulties. Self help books now generate a revenue of over 1 billion US dollars a year and anti-depressants generate one of 17 billion a year. It is strange reflection of today's world that so much profit is dependent on people being miserable.

The growing popularity of drug use means that experts expect that the rate of depression in the future will dwarf today's numbers. The easiness by which pain is avoided or pleasure induced through the use of chemicals means that more people are embracing it as a valid method of enjoying life or merely dealing with its problems. The long term effects of this on individuals and society can be quite negative. Marijuana has proven over the past few years to be much more damaging than was ever imagined. Irreversible neural damage is almost guaranteed by heavy use. Drugs designed primarily to bring happiness and bliss to the user, such as ecstasy, are renowned for causing mood problems. Short term depression is caused by mediocre amounts of use and severe long term depression the general result of extensive use. It is even possible through large amounts to completely cancel the brains ability to be happy at all. The legal drug that is alcohol has proved to be one of the most highly destructive elements in society today and has been best described as the reason why no other drug should be legalised. Ed Husain, a member of Britain's Muslim community, has wondered in his book, *The Islamist*, if conforming to the national past time of getting dangerously drunk every weekend is what people want when they ask his community to integrate.

The problems described above, as well many other social ills, can be viewed as the results of the weak conceptions of happiness people strive after today. Happiness is perceived to be available today in one of only two forms. Firstly there is the gaining of pleasure, as experienced through sexual and drug induced experiences. Also connected with this are the attempts to completely avoid all pain and suffering. What this has given birth to is the hedonistic tendencies that are an orthodox part of the West's identity today. Feeling happy is seen to be tightly tied in with pleasurable experiences. It always seems strange to those who experience happiness as something distinct and separate from this that some people have no other conception of what feeling good is.

The other form of happiness people have come to place hope in is the happiness that awaits them when all their dreams and wants are fulfilled. Consumerism may have gone a long way in promoting this childish definition of happiness but it also seems to be largely a natural delusion among human beings. Although there is an initial satisfaction when we gain something we want ultimately it leads to frustration. In terms of money it is noticeable that beyond providing for the basics there has been no proven gain between levels of happiness or satisfaction with life and the increased attainment of wealth. Increased goods and money seem to be craved for the prestige they bring about to their owner only. Even the attainment of what we want simply increases how much of it we want next time. Success in the worldly sense of the term is also often met with utter disappointment. Many people's lives could almost entirely be described as constantly striving after things, then deciding they didn't really want them after all. Some people are aware of this but have actually resigned themselves to this fate entirely and deliberately choose a target only to keep themselves busy and distracted. A lasting and real happiness, in these peoples opinion, is not possible and life goals are there just to keep people from falling into the despair this fact can bring. The treadmill is simply accepted as being the only way of life.

The hedonistic and self-obsessed lifestyle can both be connected to the nihilism that has become a prominent element in modern culture. As mentioned before, since no meaning is given for life it is assumed that no intrinsic meaning for it exists. The science that has improved the conditions of life so greatly for us is still seen as disturbing by many today as it was to the religious of the past. It seems to fit well to a life without any inherent meaning if we evolved from a blind evolutionary process. Since life has no importance then it is considered justifiable to live devoted entirely to oneself and ones desires. The unhealthy levels of self-preoccupation in modern society would not be possible if people still believed in any kind of higher power or deeper purpose. Living only for the attainment of pleasurable situations or gain in this life is another symptom of the lack of faith in any meaning outside of it. This method of dealing with the apparent hopelessness of life does not work on everyone as is reflected in the fact that suicide has now become a bigger killer throughout the world than war and murder. Another problem with this self focus is the high level of neurosis in contemporary culture. Psychotherapy and analysis flourishes because of this perception of there only being ourselves to think about. Perhaps the images of what a man or woman are expected to be glorified throughout the media also helps give rise to these feelings of inadequacy.

Those who were born before many of the recent changes in society often fail to understand younger generation's lack of ambition or drive in life. What they fail to see is how generations who were born in comfortable circumstances often see through the modern myths of society. When people are poor they believe happiness is available mainly in wealth and prestige. When people are born into these coveted conditions they realise that ideas such as this are very much mistaken. Realising this to be untrue they find it difficult in gathering the momentum to follow up on these dreams. It has actually been noticed that there is a certain guilt complex built into being born into wealthy conditions. It is likely this could be linked to what is known as the Christian guilt complex and the condemnation of riches and strange self loathing it has inspired among many Westerners.

Today the free market has become the hate target of those inhabiting the modern far left. It is usually attacked in the form of globalisation because of the increased standardisation it has brought to the world and the quiet eradication of older ways of life it has caused. It is felt as if it has trapped the people living under it in an international kill or be killed economic race. Many find it hard to integrate into this 'rat race' fully, considering that the rules that govern it appear amoral at best and that those who dominate it exude moral bankruptcy. At times it is not difficult to sympathise with this viewpoint. It is deeply unsettling that companies are now trying to form brand loyalty by developing advertising to target preschoolers (0-3 year olds). Or when considering those business men who have followed in the wake of the Iraqi invasion to make a profit from other peoples death and suffering.

The novels of Bret Easton Ellis are an interesting insight into the psychological conditions many feel the free market and liberal standards encourage. The movie adaptation of his book *The Rules of Attraction* presents all of the leads as each occupying fractured worlds. Characters share a scene but walk away with completely different conceptions of what is going on. Their self concern has made direct communication impossible and their lives are shaped only by their wants and personal desires. The wants or fears of others are no concern to them at all. His first published book *Less than Zero*, presents a picture of California youth that differs greatly from that glamorised by *The OC*. His lead finds life is not what he expected it to be but rather a vacant and aimless wandering without any real development, experience or gain. His friends can only find an escape from numbness when presented with a display of a statutory rape because of the unordinary nature of this event. Ellis' highly disturbing work *American Psycho* satirises the psychopathic nature of Wall Street economics and the 'greed is good' ethos of big business in New York. Its anti-hero Patrick Bateman works on 'murders and executions' between his daytime work on 'mergers and acquisitions'. As a raging psychopath Bateman fits in perfectly with the yuppie types he spends his days socialising with.

Chuck Palahniuk's work also displays the inherent frustrations and unease felt in modern culture. In *Fight Club* white-collar workers form underground boxing clubs and mayhem organisations to escape the boredom and limited nature of their lives. The superficiality of modern culture and experiences is lampooned throughout his work along with criticism of unrealistic advertising and the false version of life people are presented with. As his most famous character, Tyler Durden, articulating the problem perfectly, says at one point, 'Our great war is a spiritual one, our great Depression our lives'. Something else he criticises is the atomised individual's constant search for recognition through fame. The covering up of the harsh and painful realities of life is a practise he points out as hopelessly naïve and misguided. Any kind of satisfaction or real enjoyment in life for these characters is completely out of the question.

The life focused nature of secular society has meant that there is a dangerous, but growing, orthodoxy of denying the reality of death. The religious acceptance of death as an inevitable and important element of life has been completely jettisoned for denial or fantasies of genetic or cryogenic immortality. The old ceremonies and gatherings that helped loved ones accept their grief has also disappeared into quick and hushed funeral arrangements. It has become a subject few are willing to raise in conversation or face up to without feeling fear or despair. It is natural that in such an individualistic society this would be the case, considering death means the end of that which we value most. It could also be connected to how it is the one major flaw in the plan for life inherent within a modern capitalist democratic framework. Ultimately what is the point of consuming so many goods or making so much money if you are going to die and leave it all behind?

Another attitude that has grown to new heights with modern times is that of cynicism. The discoveries of the Enlightenment have made it impossible for Christianity to regain the position it once held over the people of Europe. To fill this emptiness new meanings for life were cobbled together. All claimed to be perfectly scientific and were mostly Enlightenment orientated. Many realised they were no more than rehashes of the Judaeo-Christian heritage and shuddered at the dystopian nightmares they threatened to create. The whole world watched as each of these suggestions crashed and were revealed to have brought murder and misery to millions. It is revealing to remember that not only did they collapse but that they were also entirely wrong, whether in their scientific analysis or economic theories. There is no evidence of the primitive communistic society Marx said preceded our own and there are no different species within humanity as the social Darwinists claimed. These are within the realm of a weak kind of myth. With the religion that infused every area of Western civilization becoming impossible to believe in and every attempted alternative to it falling in disaster it has left those living today with a certain amount of cynicism. Should any political leader rise up in today's world with a plan of social action that he promises would cure all our problems it is unlikely any of us would believe him, even if he did claim scientific backing. In actual fact it is hard for us to believe that there was once a time when millions did believe such characters.

When people do appear to apply themselves to some cause or belief system today it is often met with surprise or patronising incredulousness. Some of today's movements deserve such scepticism, such as the use of defunct Western political salvation in Islamism or the multi-national corporative structure of Scientology, but many appear to attack believers only because they now find it impossible to believe themselves. Atheists and other kinds of non-believers smugly wonder how it is that those who do believe in something are so blind to not see the reality of the world's meaninglessness before them. They claim to be the ultimate realists but have actually come to represent a brand of miserable pessimism. A brand that seems to feel that any kind of happiness or enjoyment of life must be linked to some delusion or false beliefs. Often those who continue to believe in a higher meaning and cause in life are quiet and hesitant in their beliefs out of fear of ridicule.

This cynicism has become something many have learnt to accept in themselves. The truth that we have come to realise is that there is no social plan or political agenda that can solve the problems humanity faces. Alongside with this cynicism is our acceptance of nihilism and of the life of distraction and short term pleasures that is needed to placate it. Instead of crying out in despair at the thought of life being without higher value many of us seem to be trying to live without thinking about it. Or alternatively trying to get the most amount of good times shoved into it as possible, considering that existential meaninglessness appears to be nothing compared to the suffering of existential boredom.

The Sword From The Scabbard

Friedrich Nietzsche was born in 1844, near Leipzig in Germany. He is important here because his life story and thoughts capture the changes Western civilization has endured in the past few centuries perfectly. Nietzsche lived at a time when a new kind of priest, the philosopher, was coming to dominate the European intellectual scene. He was the son of a clergyman and so was raised within the standard Christian world view, which impressed him so much that he decided he wanted to emulate his father when he grew up. He was generally considered a happy, but highly intense, child. His plans on serving God for a living came to nothing when his beliefs were shattered by the release of Darwin's hypothesis on the origin of species. A world that still frightens many today, with its barrenness and moral emptiness, revealed itself to him and us through his writings.

Nietzsche lamented that he was born before his time and that his writings would not be understood by those around him. Some of his work would in fact be doctored by his anti-Semitic sister and used by her to help legitimise the Nazi movement. He predicted the massive upheavals and wars of the twentieth century, knowing that human moral development would not be able to keep up with technological advancement. It has almost been taboo among certain circles to announce any influence by Nietzsche since Hitler named him as his favourite philosopher.

Nietzsche recognised all of the followings of his day as little more than Christian corruptions destined to failure. The materialistic culture of distraction that keeps many in the West busy today was something that amused him, but he never took seriously as a way some people would actually spend their lives doing. Much of his work appears to be a recoil from Christianity and all of the movements it spawned. He was especially virulent towards its conception of morals, which he considered a slave morality that prevented some people from reaching their noble potential. Nietzsche wanted to be sure of escaping Christianity entirely and seeing what he could come up with about the world. He was influenced by scientific discovery but not by the scientism that had gripped so many of his contemporaries. Where he disagreed mostly with scientist's description of the universe is where they described it as being like machine. This was not so he believed. A machine has a job which gives it purpose, which is a quality the universe appears to lack.

His attack on Christian belief and psychology was especially devastating and probably reflects the suffering his loss of faith brought upon himself. He was not concerned with theological or scientific arguments for dismissing God but with how the new scientific ethos had made it impossible to believe in Him. The dismissal of God was not accompanied with joy or satisfaction, however, but with great anguish and pain. Something that had probably comforted him throughout his younger life, such as when his father died in 1849, Nietzsche now had to let go of.

He once described humanity as a kind of disease making its way across the skin of the Earth. He wanted people to understand how much the new discoveries about the world alter the way in which it is understood to work. The illusions of progress and humanities natural goodness and ability incensed him so much that he wanted people to understand how ultimately insignificant they were. The rise and fall of mankind would be less than a flash compared to the span of the universe. He believed we needed a new way of viewing and living life in order to reflect this reality.

It would begin with his new conception of morality. Instead of the old slave morality inherited by Christianity it was to be a new noble morality more fitting with the laws of the universe. Out went silly things like compassion and love, which only slowed the best men down, and in came values of ruthlessness and superiority. The only justification for humanity Nietzsche could compile would be the emergence of a new kind of being. This 'superman' (ubermensch) was to look back on contemporary humanity in the same way we look at apes. We would be a focus of ridicule and embarrassment to the new strong mankind. He would be in complete control of his mind and actions and lord it over all the others who were weaker than himself. For Nietzsche the 'will to power' was the driving force in the universe and must be grasped after to justify existence.

It is not difficult to see which parts of his philosophy Hitler felt compelled by. Joy and happiness were only to be found in increasing the amount of power we had over the world. He once described happiness charmingly, as the 'only thing in the world that did not require any justification' because 'it is its own justification.' It is only a pity how terrible the road he pointed to it was.

Many people see philosophy as a dry and abstract subject of little worth or influence. This is only because they can only see the actions in the world and not the influences behind them. Men and women who have spent their time deep in thought and learning have shaped world events. An obvious case would be Marx and the influence his critique of capitalism would have on the future communists. Or Adam Smith, the visionary of the free market. Thinkers with a more subtle reputation would be likes of Hayek or Freidman and the influences they had on Thatcherism. Nietzsche may have not become the 'ubermensch' or taken part in the upheavals he predicted, but that did not stop others from attempting to do so. In a very real way Nietzsche could be considered the figure who gave birth to the 20th century.

In a way his predictions of war and destruction were self-fulfilling prophecies. Hitler and many of the Nazi's would have considered themselves to be this new race of supermen. Their policies certainly reflected such a belief. The movements promotion of brutality and might is right philosophy would indicate an acceptance of Nietzsche's new morality albeit based on vulgar simplifications of it.

Nietzsche collapsed into a kind of mental paralysis towards the end of his life. Between 1889 and 1900, the year he died, he was taken care of by his sister. No one is certain why or how this happened to him but the incident that first provoked it is curious. He spotted a man whipping his horse, causing the creature great pain, and ran towards it to intervene. Just as he wrapped his arms around the creature to protect it his mind collapsed and never regained itself.

It is ironic, given the advice he laid before humanity, that this should be his last sane act. It is also amusing that during his travels a landlady nicknamed him the little saint because of his impeccable manners. His writings, both in style and content, make deeply fascinating reading. His psychological insights and musings on human nature still cause the reader to consider truths about themselves that can be difficult to understand or face up to. His work on the nature of knowledge and conventional morality is convincing, but his prescription of how to live and behave in this world was irresponsible and most likely the result of his own weaknesses. There is little doubt that he had himself in mind when advocating this new form of humanity. He may have felt that his sensitive nature and shy conduct had caused him nothing but pain in his life and that if he was a hard and cold overlord events such as the death of his father would not have hurt him as much. It is a disturbing fact that a mind like Nietzsche's considered human kinds place in the world and this was the best justification he could come up for it. The 'ubermensch', however, should be relegated to history. It is a monstrosity that has had its chance and shown its worth. What we can take from this mans work is a deep encouragement to think differently to the accepted norms. He was too astute to fall into the trap of endorsing a corruption of Christianity, and reached completely outside that context instead. What he came up with was unattractive, but deeply original for his time, and in that sense he is to be admired.

Nietzsche is considered to be one of the first of the Existentialist philosophers. This school negates any outside meaning to life and contends that it is up to the individual to create meaning to their lives. Other members of the movement into the 20th century included Jean-Paul Sartre and Albert Camus. The title of Sartre's novel *Nausea* captures the feeling provoked when man considers his isolation in the cosmos. The dread, boredom and absurdness of existence in a meaningless world play a major part in their work. An interesting point of this philosophy is its description of the despair that derives from trying to live and make choices in a world of which our understanding is incomplete and uncertain.

It is directions such as this that modern Western thought has now travelled. Just as those who are not aware of the connection between Adam Smith and the free market there are those who do not see the influences these thinkers and philosophers have had upon the modern world. Many see the free market as a natural phenomenon rather than the development of numerous historical occurrences and political arrangements. Our sense of life devoted towards ourselves and our personal goals are in a large way derived from Existentialism and the image of ourselves as being alone and unsure in the universe.

The development of philosophical thought in the modern era has travelled in strange and elusive directions. If post-modernism has not confused enough people post-postmodernism just might. The intellectuals of the West sometimes seem to be constantly trying only to confound one another. Few, if any, of their suggestions seem to offer any comfort or even any clear answers to the mysteries humanity is faced with. Of course, to expect such a thing leaves us open to accusations of desiring relief or comfort over truth (If such a thing even exists in the accuser's particular school). Whilst philosophy of the past was designed to give advice and guidance to people, today's version of it seems to value itself in being as far away from daily human experience as possible.

The counter cultural myth today still plays a large influence on how people view society. This belief in a powerful and greedy establishment that can only be escaped through alternate culture continues to inspire new counter cultural movements. These movements portray mainstream culture as corrupt and superficial and that the only way to overcome them is to drop out completely or accept some other, more 'real' culture. Today it is consumerist society that is perceived in this negative way, whether in terms of modern music or clothes. Unfortunately for modern alternate movements this establishment of a counter culture opens up a brand new market to drive consumerist society further forward. Today the mainstream is dependent upon the forming of counter cultural movements. Kurt Cobain did not understand this when his music became popular and he thought that it had entered the mainstream and so betrayed its counter cultural roots. He committed suicide in response.

This way of viewing the world derives from the 1960's and the liberal overreach fed by the fascist trauma of Nazi Germany. As mentioned earlier all areas of authority were attacked as oppression and the rules normally governing protocol and behaviour were weakened. For example the once accepted protocol of approaching members of the opposite sex have almost entirely been abolished, giving rise to the rule less and awkward nature of instigating relationships today. Instead of perceiving the rules of male and female interaction as designed to ease and make comfortable the opening process of initiating a relationship feminists saw all such rules as evidence of patriarchal oppression. This has also been held responsible for the growth of yob culture among young males. Today books that offer tips on correct behaviour in situations such as these often make bestsellers.

 A similar attitude was launched against other areas of authority and dismissed their rules as signs of oppression. It is not only relationship books that sell well but any book offering advice on how to live or behave. Attempts to free the people from oppression have left millions without any kind of established guidelines on behaviour in certain situations. It is true that many of the old rules concerning behaviour were stifling, but to dismiss them without any kind of replacement has only added to the modern sense of alienation. So as well as existentialist philosophy leaving us alone and without guidance, because of the counter cultural myth the rules of social interaction have done the same.

 Atheism throughout history has shown itself to be a temporary and transient outlook. In whatever tradition it has risen in it has disappeared when the conditions that gave rise to it are addressed. The term atheist has no objective meaning or definition but is dependent upon contemporary conceptions of divinity. It arises because of inadequate religious concepts and disappears when more sufficient understandings emerge. The dry and unimaginative Christian atheism thinkers like Dawkins espouse as a replacement for religion is a feeble basis for living. Any kind of motive in life must stand on its own two legs instead of being defined by its opposition to another creed. The transitory nature of atheism would also mean that it something people can only hold for a short time before it strains.

 Some still maintain that religion will never have an influence over people ever again and that science will reveal all we can and will ever know about the universe. The nature of science means that its answers are entirely cerebral and deeply unsatisfying since they do not sit with our subjective experience of reality. It can tell us that the universe may be shaped like a doughnut but this nothing has to do with how we should act in our daily lives. The answers are all given quickly as well, encouraging people to expect all of their questions to have tidy, clear and immediate answers. *The Hitchhikers Guide To The Galaxy* displays this point amusingly, with the answer to life, the universe and everything being the number 42. If science could come up with a response for such a question it would be something in this category of answer. What anyone expects to be done with such an answer is the real mystery. The sciences have also diverged into different subjects, each of which has an explanation of the world based only in its own particular branch. An answer that can bring all of these together into one explanation would appear to now be impossible. Nietzsche had it right when he declared that the emphasis on purely scientific knowledge had made wisdom impossible to attain. The discoveries of science have no end or discernable final goal while wisdom sought to bring about a wholeness and understanding in its holder. No matter what scientific knowledge is discovered it has little bearing on our beliefs or values.

Overall, the West today is deeply confused about its identity and beliefs. Of course, many within it claim to see things clearly, but more often than not they have closed their belief systems to analysis or challenge. There is a hesitance and reluctance among thinkers to probe into the truth too far out of fear that the answers that await are the worst that are expected. What if the universe really is completely Godless and pointless and humanity is just a momentary phenomenon? What if Nietzsche was right and the 'will to power' is at the centre of reality, forming a heart of darkness? Happiness would seem impossible with this as its background. From the way society has now structured itself it would appear it has already accepted this. Since this life is the only one hedonism and self advancement have been accepted as the norm. Narcissism has been almost cultivated like a virtue, spawning entire populations who do little but think or talk about themselves.

Many, when asked thoughts on religion, give an answer that they believe in something, but not religion. An answer that reflects a deep level of self involvement. This something they shape in their own minds to suit themselves and their personal goals and so long as their something does not interfere in their lives by restricting their behaviour or challenging their wants they can hold onto it.

In actual fact this is also what many claiming to be conventionally religious do. God is used as an excuse to justify their personal desires rather than to challenge them. This is not belief or faith but rather a theology that justifies self aggrandisement. I have even heard some Christians argue that if God created them, then he created their wants, so they are entirely right in pursuing them.

With mainly empty and weak forms of religion, self obsession, nihilism or existential tiredness at hand the West has reached a point of deep concern. It is impossible to be sure of where it will travel in now but the ongoing growth of fundamentalist Christianity would indicate the basic direction. Those who are dismayed by such a prospect should be aware that for some time a post-secular society has been spotted on the horizon. That is not to say that Christianity will dominate the future as it has the past, but that existential angst will find a cure for itself. The question is if there is a cure that we can accept without deluding ourselves or rejecting the admirable values that have developed as a part of today's society.

The Sword From The Scabbard

4

THE AWAKENED ONE

Many see the problems of disillusionment, nihilism and existential boredom as uniquely modern. Indeed, the specific emergence and manifestations of them are unique to today, but the core emotions and suffering associated with them are as old as humanity. There are several known stages in recorded history in which people have complained to suffer the same kind of malaise and anomie. Ancient tablets from Mesopotamia and Egypt display a similar dismay with received knowledge and fear of what its abandonment meant. What it is that provoked this is impossible to know. It could have been the popularity of new knowledge which dramatically challenged the common worldview, thereby robbing their lives of meaning. Or it could have been something inherent within the traditions themselves that led to its own collapse. It is a mix of both these factors that has caused the current crisis in the West.

The time of discontent that we know most about occurred just before and early in what we call the Axial Age. It spans from 800 until 200 BCE and centred in areas of Greece, present day Israel, India and China. We call it the Axial Age because most of the views and ideas that circulate the world today derive from this time. The conception of the world being involved in a struggle between good and evil was laid down by Zarathustra, a holy man from present day Iran. Aware of this, when Nietzsche challenged conventional morality he wrote of Zarathustra coming down to tell the people he had been mistaken before and had a new morality for them. His ideas of a battle between good and evil would also involve a saviour figure to redeem humanity. The faith Zarathustra founded, Zoroastrianism, still exists in Iran. The dichotomy, so much a part of it, has influenced the modern world deeply. In other parts of the world thinkers and teachers composed ideas that would be used to shape the future. The roots of all the monotheistic faiths were laid down by the prophets of the Israelites both in exile and in Israel. The ancient Greek philosophers developed the roots of what would become science and rational thought. Confucius and Lao Tzu, in China, would develop systems of ethical thought and philosophy that would come to dominate Chinese society before being disseminated around the world. Very little of what we know today was not touched upon or considered by the great thinkers and leaders of this time.

No one is quite sure what led to this golden age of discovery and knowledge or what provoked it to occur in such diverse regions of the world but it may have something to do with the disappearance of old political boundaries and the imposition of new ones. As they were altered and the certainties they stood for disappeared it would have shaken people's sense of place in the world. These structures would have touched upon all of these regions and as they and all of the beliefs associated with them withdrew explanations would have been sought. With old certainties and ways of life no longer relevant people were free to seek new ones. Now Greece would produce some of the most important minds to influence Western thought. Socrates advised his students to question everything and admitted that he knew nothing for certain. Plato formed the foundations of Western utopian thinking with his ideal of the philosopher king and a perfect society. The prophets of Israel are responsible for the ethical natures of Judaism, Christianity and Islam. The call for obedience before God and the need to take care of the sick and weak were composed during the Axial Age. It was the Jewish welfare system that largely caused them to be admired by the Romans. The main elements of the philosophical Upanishads and the beautiful *Bhagavad-Gita* (Divine Song) would become increasingly popular in India, giving an identity and definition to the huge following we know today as Hinduism. The realist philosophy behind Lao Tzu's Taoism and Confucianism, other than shaping Chinese civilization, is still today considered valid and realistic advice. Business sections in book stores often have copies of Lao Tzu's *The Art of War* for sale. All of these innovative thinkers developed new ways to deal with life and the dislocation from it that can arise. Their messages often became blurred with time and conventionalising. The core points they would try and get across would become lost when their messages were turned into mere custom. Instead of the escape from traditional thought and liberation they taught their names and influence would be used to form new conventions, containing none of the movement's original meaning, and stifle most truly independent thought. Of this, it is unfortunately true that Christianity is probably the best example.

The single most influential and possibly most original thinker known from these times was born in the Himalayan foothills, in what is present day Nepal. Like many of those around him he would be struck by the seemingly pointless and painful nature of life and seek answers to the human condition. When he lived the sense of humanity being lost and desperate for real answers had reached fever pitch. Unlike today, when many are ready to accept a life of distraction or be absorbed into traditions they know are flawed, the people of this time encouraged and supported practitioners searching for new answers. He recognised the problem as being entirely spiritual in nature, rather than materialistically political or particularly cultural, and sought answers from this realm. He knew received wisdom could not be entirely trusted so put into practise and tested everything he learnt himself. In the end answers are what he found and taught. By the time he died, around the age of 80, after a 45 year teaching mission he had founded a movement that would become the first world religion. It is ironic that it persisted so strongly when he only expected it to last a few hundred years at most.

Most iconography displaying him has him sitting alone, but we know that most of his life he was surrounded by huge crowds of people eager to see and learn from him. The changes in society when he was alive that caused the loss of place and confidence among the population are not dissimilar from our own. The old caste system had been challenged by the rise of a new merchant class in the cities and other busy regions. The religious structures of the time were dependent on this caste system so when it lost meaning so did they. An example of this was that there was a caste especially made for priests and scholars. This class, known as the Brahmin, would intercede between the power behind the universe and the other classes through the medium of ritual. With the disintegration of this system how were people supposed to communicate or interact with the divine. People were left needing a new thought system or explanation for how they should live in the world

The modern rise of the free market has caused a similar sense of dislocation from the past. The old cultural norms and behaviours that were once taken for granted have now given way to crass materialism and self promotion. The rise of the merchant class meant that individualism and self reliance became increasingly important. Any religious solutions to the problems would have to include these values. The similarity between the crises is probably what makes the teachings of this movement especially applicable to today. It is important to note that the teachings of this movement declare themselves as universal, rather than being contained to any particular circumstance or place. The teachings reveal truths about what it means to be human and laid out a path that its founder understood as the goal of human life.

He was born with the name Siddhartha Gautama into a tribe known as the Sakyans. They were formed into a small republic and ruled over by a council. This council would have been maintained by the richest families and leadership determined by a rota. The political arrangements Siddhartha grew up in would influence how he organised and treated his future followers. The times Siddhartha grew up in were harshly violent and destructive. The withdrawal of the ancient empires had created a kind of dark age with tyrants and kings struggling for power and control over the various regions of the Ganges. When he lived it would seem as if the type of republics he was raised in were in their twilight. Towards the end of his own life his tribe were decimated by invaders. The violence of the age was another issue that concerned the people of this time. The unleashing of aggressive force and destruction often poisons society as it seeps hatred and grudges down to every level. Given the conditions of the world he was born into Siddhartha's mission and accomplishments are often hard to believe.

The received stories about Siddhartha's life are, like Jesus', mainly hagiographical. To remove the more miraculous or extraordinary elements from them is to miss the point the writers were attempting to make. Being a psychologically astute movement his biographers would have used the tools of mythology carefully. When confronted with the evil god Mara for example, we are to understand this as a manifestation of his own delusional thoughts. Even some of the traditional details of his early life are to be read in this way. Once understood the skilful work that goes into the composition of hagiographies is both an impressive and highly satisfying method of transmitting knowledge.

In the 19th century some scholars doubted he existed at all but today few would take this view seriously. The nature and consistency of the received teachings points to a single mind and origination and although we can never be certain about some of the more detailed accounts of his life the basic contour of it is most certainly true. The story of his life would later come to be mixed with his teachings in order to make both easier to understand, so that it would not only convey what happened in his life but also what his life meant. In the end the hagiography has not only allowed us to discern his teachings more clearly but given us a good idea of what actually happened to him.

Historical research would not have the same devastating effect here as it has on Christianity anyway. Even if it were proved that he had not existed at all it would not affect the movement that descended from him today. The cornerstone of Christian faith is the divinity of the historical Jesus. It stands or falls on this issue. The cornerstone of the movement Siddhartha would go on to found stands on the truth or falsity of its teachings. If the way of life that he set does not reach the goals it claims to then it fails. The test of truth is whether or not it works, not if the stories surrounding it are true or not. It could be said in this movement that its teachings are situated in the same place as

Christ is to Christianity. No study of its past or foundations can have much effect on how it is perceived or practised.

We are told that Siddhartha was born and raised in the best possible conditions. His father, Suddhodana, is described as being greatly wealthy and in a position of power. The legends describe him as a king but as we know Siddhartha was born into a republic. If his father was in a position of power he was most likely on the governing council or else its leader. Later in life Siddhartha would mix quite easily with members of the ruling caste, indicating that it is most likely true he lived in good conditions since he had experience of their kind of life. This would mean that he was born into what corresponded to the ksatriya caste, comprised of noblemen and warriors.

On his birth soothsayers and wise men were consulted to give Suddhodana an idea of what the future might hold for his son. They predicted that his child would become one of two things. He would either become a great world leader and ruler of men (Cakkavati) or else he would renounce the household life entirely but awaken to the full potential of humanity (Buddha). Suddhodana decided his son would, like him, become a ruler of men and set about making sure this would happen.

The willpower, determination and strength of character that shines through Siddhartha's life story indicate that he would have made an admirable political leader. At a time his home and people were under threat from the growing kingdoms of Magadha and Kosala nearby. Siddhartha's father probably desired greatly for his son to become a capable and strong ruler. The image of and temptation to become a Cakavatti plagued Siddhartha's mind throughout his search for spiritual answers. More generally it can be compared to the power fantasies that are latent in the minds of most people. We imagine ourselves being strong and admired by others and many of us go to huge lengths to reach such goals. Realising the pointlessness of and defeating this kind of empty fantasy would play a large part in the teachings Siddhartha would develop.

Suddhodana conspired with those who worked for him to prevent his son from encountering anything that would turn him away from the path of a cakavatti. This meant hiding from him things that might make him go into the wilderness and seek answers to the problems of life. The way of doing this, Suddhodana decided upon, was to hide all of life's inherent difficulties from Siddhartha. It was decided that the child would never want for anything and would never have to encounter any kind of pain that would make him question the nature of his life. This meant Siddhartha would grow up surrounded with every available luxury and with his every desire being fulfilled. His father had all signs of suffering and pain removed from his view wherever he travelled so that even by the time he was a grown man he knew nothing of the pains that afflicted life. Unfortunately, this meant that for most of his youth he had to be confined within the walls of his father's palaces, of which there were several throughout the kingdom. Siddhartha married the beautiful daughter of a neighbouring king, Yashodara, and eventually she gave him a son, Rahula. Suddhodana was pleased and decided his plans had worked perfectly.

Throughout this, not unexpectedly, Siddhartha developed an overwhelming curiosity about the world that existed outside the walls of his pleasure palace. When he was near the age of thirty he convinced a servant to assist him sneaking out and seeing the outside world. When he encountered a man wrecked by disease Siddhartha was shocked and asked his servant what this meant. The servant, Channa, explained how everyone in their lives would become sick at some point, just as this man was. No one could escape such a condition forever. Siddhartha was horrified at the thought that those he loved or he himself could be struck down by such a condition, and the happiness his sheltered life gave him suddenly disappeared. How could he return to the life he lived before knowing that this awaited all the people around him. Siddhartha returned to the palace but unable to settle, snuck out with Channa again. This time they saw an old man, something Siddhartha had never encountered before. When it was explained to him that this was the fate of all who lived long enough he was shocked. How could people spend their lives chasing after beauty for themselves and from others when it would always disappear with time? How could people value such things with this knowledge? He returned to the palace again, more disturbed than ever before. On his next visit outside the walls, he and Channa saw a dead body. Again he asked his servant what it meant.

The Sword From The Scabbard

Channa explained how this was the fate of all living things without exception. No matter how hard one tries or how far they travel they will never escape the reality of death. With the knowledge that not only would he and his family suffer, but that one day they would die and lose everything, Siddhartha was devastated.

How could it be possible to enjoy life fully in the knowledge that it would all end before long. Why was humanity trapped in such a condition? Sickness, old age and death seemed to rob life of its meaning, revealing instead a prison of pain and pointlessness. Again Siddhartha snuck out of the palace but this time he saw something that gave him hope. Walking through the centre of a busy marketplace he spotted a man travelling quietly, carrying only a bowl for food. Struck by the mans calm nature and the sense of determination emanating from him, Siddhartha approached and asked him who he was and what he was doing. The man explained how he had renounced the life of a householder and had gone out to seek the truth behind human existence. He, and thousands like him, had set themselves the goal of developing a way of life that would offer people the escape from these sufferings. Siddhartha was struck by this and decided immediately that this was the only way he could go on living in the world. The life of a householder now became impossible for him to return to. The trivial nature of its daily activities appeared like nothing compared to what these wanderers were on the way to discovering. His desire to find a cure to life's pain was not a selfish one, but motivated out of his wish that he would be able to provide those around him with some kind of relief from the inevitable pains of sickness and mortality.

He approached his father and asked him for permission to leave the palace and live as one of these homeless wanderers. Like most fathers would, Suddhodana reacted with anger and disbelief. Not only did his only son want to become what he saw as a beggar, but somehow all of his plans had failed. He denied his son the request and tried to prevent him from leaving the palace. One night Siddhartha prepared himself secretly and made ready to leave. He did not even wake his wife and child to say goodbye, perhaps afraid he would not be able to make himself leave if he did. Instead he awoke Channa and they left silently in the darkness. When they had went far enough

The Sword From The Scabbard

Siddhartha gave his jewellery to Channa and told him to return it to the palace. It was only now Channa realised what his master was intending and what he had helped him do. He became upset and asked what he should tell the rest of the family. Siddhartha said to tell them that he did not leave because he doesn't love them, but because he does love them. He explained how he had now set out to seek a method of overcoming sickness, old age and death and that if he ever discovered such a thing he would return to teach them it. Channa could do nothing but return to the palace and Siddhartha set out on his journey.

Along with giving us some idea of what went through Siddhartha's mind to motivate his search the story of his younger life is mixed with astute psychological insights. Of course, it is ridiculous to believe literally that someone could grow to this age and remain so unaware of the realities of sickness and death. Instead the stories real meaning is much more subtle and realistic. The pleasure palace is used as a representation of the response many make when faced with life. They seek to insulate themselves from its hurtful aspects by surrounding themselves only with what they like or desire. In a real way we all inhabit palaces of this kind. Our lives are shaped around only that which we want to encounter and think about. It is carefully guarded to avoid the intrusion of elements of life we might refer to as depressing or gloomy. The walls of this palace can be built from practically anything. In the hedonistic culture of today drugs, alcohol and sex are all used as tools to reinforce the walls that divide our subjective experience of life from the harsh realities that hang over it. Others focus entirely upon day to day tasks to keep themselves busy and distracted so as not to allow their thoughts to travel in such directions. The pleasure palace is a great metaphor for a mind in a complete state of denial. It does not even want to know about the realities of life never mind being prepared to find some way of accepting them.

The effort Suddhodana puts into protecting his son comes to nothing as will all attempts to avoid life's suffering. At some point it will break through and just as in Siddhartha's case, if we are not prepared for it the effects can be devastating. Even in cases where people are prepared, suffering is often disorientating and difficult to accept. It is often hard for many to even admit that they are suffering when it does come along. Siddhartha's discovery of sickness, old age and death made the daily activities and chores of life impossible. He wondered how people could live such a life in knowledge of what awaited them and the answer was in his own past. People live in pleasure palaces such as he did, but theirs is normally of their own devising. Just like his, however, they can only last for a certain amount of time before the walls begin to crack.

Perhaps there is some literal truth in Siddhartha only realising these facts at this age. It is one thing to know that we are all going to die at the back of our minds, but it is a different thing to face up to it. To truly realise the meaning of death and how it can strike without warning can at times be overwhelming. The way in which the world goes on, only without us, leaves us feeling panicked and isolated. Most days we can operate without thinking about the fact that everyone around us will one day die, but when it does seep in life itself seems to stand still for a moment. Although the path Siddhartha would discover is today followed by millions, the fact is that the majority of the world's inhabitants will never leave their palaces. They will never allow death and suffering to truly enter their conscious vision and feel the life transforming effects they bring. Instead most of us will allow ourselves to become palace enclosed Siddhartha's until death.

The homeless wanderer Siddhartha met on his trip outside the palace walls was a representative of the feverish search for a way to overcome suffering and pain that had gripped this part of the world at the time. All over the Ganges Plain and parts of India seekers and teachers had wandered teaching various ways of living (dharma) they claimed were the best for humanity. India today still remains the world's most religious country and has a long tradition of supporting and admiring these spiritual seekers. Thousands of young men would wander the countryside seeking out these teachers and their various dharmas. Often people would move from one to another and talk about the merits and demerits of each. Many of these teachers were a part of larger schools of thought. The Materialists, led by Ajira, believed the physical world was all that really existed. In the end we were all a part of the rubbish heap, so they advised everyone to do whatever they wanted with their lives. They would fit well in some parts of today's culture. They dismissed any ideas of a soul or life force and held that when death arrived it was the complete annihilation of the individual. The Skeptics, led by Sanjaya, denied the existence of any final truth to reality. For them knowledge was only used to advance ones position and any final answers could not be found to life, because they did not exist. Most schools differed from this, however, and were something similar to what we know as Hinduism.

 In this system permeating the entire universe was a benevolent and powerful force known as Brahman. It was this that all the other gods and goddesses were manifestations of, as it resided in all things. A part of it existed within each human being and was known as the Self (atman), opposed to the smaller day to day self we mistake ourselves being. It was buried beneath many layers of this smaller self that the real Self lay and the goal in human life, they maintained, was to discover this Self within ourselves, thereby becoming absorbed into Brahman. It would be only then that we would be awakened to our full humanity. In Christian terms this could be described as the soul merging with God. It was here that the overcoming of suffering truly lay. Merging with Brahman meant entering a state of mind indescribably blissful and immune to the pain and suffering in the world. It was not as if there would be no pain or death anymore, but rather that it was now easy to accept and live with because of the joy, confidence and strength granted by this state. Unlike Christianity, however, these people maintained that this state was to be reached within this life but with only great effort. Even at the time Siddhartha had lived the techniques of yoga and meditation were ancient in this part of the world. Men had developed ways of controlling and developing their minds ordinary people could scarcely imagine. It was taken for granted that these techniques could unlock powers and mental abilities that normally lie dormant in humanity, but for even the most gifted and accomplished practitioner merging with Brahman was still an immense task. What the many thousands of seekers in Siddhartha's time were looking for was the true way to uncover and discover the Self that lay at the core of their being. Each teacher's methodology would be measured against others on this criteria alone. It was learning techniques and philosophy from some of these movements that Siddhartha would begin his mission.

Siddhartha's first teacher was a man called Alara Kalama. Like most of his contemporaries his path led to the discovery of the Self. Kalama had been taught this method years before and since he had excelled at it stayed on to teach others. When Siddhartha met him he had become the lead teacher of this particular dharma. Kalama accepted him as a student and proceeded to teach him what he knew and how he could experience it himself.

An important element of the kind of knowledge that was taught in these circles was the way in which it transcended the intellect. Ordinary logical discourse and conversation can only pierce knowledge and truth so far. What was taught by men like Kalama was direct experience of truths that could not be experienced by the cerebral facilities alone. The truth and existence of the Self, especially, could not be argued rationally, but only experienced directly. This is where many find religion difficult to understand and accept. They do not understand that there are area's of knowledge that cannot be discerned through rational and logical discourse. As we all know religious and spiritual truths are not always coherent or sensible, but that does not mean that they are always untrue. These kinds of truth do not defy reason, but transcend it. Another area of human endeavour that employs a similar use of knowledge is the arts. Asking purely logical and rational questions of a painting or a poem would be seen as folly; just as taking a poem only literally would close it of to all deeper analysis. These things touch us at levels much deeper and fundamental to our humanity than the intellect. Since the advent of the Enlightenment and its primacy on rationality we have found it difficult to accept the existence of this kind of truth. Our mindsets naturally tend to reject all that does not correspond to purely logical discourse since we believe that if something is not rational then it cannot be true. This attitude mainly serves us well when we reject things which are pre-rational, but makes no room for understanding the things we encounter which are trans-rational.

Siddhartha was now being taught methods of how to align his view of the world, by taking control of and altering his consciousness. Meditative and yogic techniques would quieten his own mind and all of the subjective views that came with it which blocked his vision of the true nature of reality. By filtering the world thus, he would see it as it really was, and the Self would be revealed to him.

Eventually Siddhartha was guided to this point by Kalama and experienced the place he was told would reveal the Self. This state of mind was indescribable to people who had no direct experience of it. It could only be explained to others in purely negative terms since it was entirely unlike anything we experience in daily life. It could not be compared to anything, only described in terms of what it was not. Some attempted to describe it as entering a room and finding nothing there. Not a void, but something unexpected and beyond mundane description. Words, literally, could not do it justice.

Other inward looking mystical traditions have often described the final point on their journey as being something similar to this. Jews reflect the indescribable nature of the final reality by not spelling out its name fully in texts, but rather as G-d. This realm of being transcended the world we knew so the rules we take for granted need not apply to it. An important example of this is the rules concerning existence and non-existence. If it transcended this universe and its rules then it cannot be described as existing or not existing in the way things within the universe do. This may go a long way in explaining why one person could never communicate to another this knowledge. It had to be experienced for oneself. How could a person describe in words something that both does and does not exist? This also makes many of the debates concerning the existence or non-existence of God in the West appears misguided. If the reality referred to as God is beyond the walls of the universe then it can do both. Islamic mystical traditions also employ techniques designed to propel the seeker on an inner journey to altered consciousness. It is often remarked upon when the goal is reached how one both does and does not see the face of Allah. It is interesting to note that all accounts of it agree on its benevolent and blissful nature. It is this same place Siddhartha was led to as the goal of Kalama's dharma.

When Siddhartha explained to Kalama that he had reached this place Kalama was ecstatic. He explained to Siddhartha how he wanted him now to stay and help him teach others what he had discovered. Siddhartha, however, could not. What he had just been through, he decided, was not what he was looking for. Elements of the philosophical system and the nature of the experience had left him doubting this path was the release from suffering he had vowed to discover. He wondered how what he had experienced could be the eternal and pure Self when he knew he had produced the experience himself. Did it really exist within everyone or was it only created when he threw in such effort and willpower? A larger problem for Siddhartha concerned the transitory nature of the experience. This state of mind he entered into had been beautifully blissful, but when it was over he would still always return to the world of pain and suffering. Siddhartha left the dharma of Alara Kalama and continued his search.

He stayed within a similar philosophical background when he adopted for a time the dharma of Uddaka Ramapatta. Again the search was on for the Self that lay hidden beneath the murky layers of the conscious mind. Ramapatta explained how he had discovered a realm beyond that of the nothingness. Herein lay the true Self. It was a realm described as being beyond all perception and non-perception. Ramapatta explained that this was the Self that meant release from the pains of life. Again Siddhartha disagreed. When he managed to reach this point he still retained all of the questions and concerns that he had before. Again, this could not be the real Self since he had brought about the experience himself and again, he returned to the world of suffering and pain when the experience was over. What Siddhartha sought was something that would stay with the practitioner always and no matter what. Otherwise it would not be the true overcoming of pain and suffering since it could not be depended on. At this time he also would have developed doubts about the doctrine of the eternal Self altogether. He may have begun to wonder at this time if it was possible that this unchanging and central part of the human being existed at all. Whether or not he was able to answer this at the time, Siddhartha decided to change his approach anyway.

Outside of Maghada there lay a forest where the most extreme ascetics were known to gather. Siddhartha decided to go there and join them. Asceticism denied the practitioner any kind of comfort or ease in daily life, but rather the deliberate courting of pain and hardship. It was thought that this would enable the practitioner to take control over their senses by developing and strengthening their willpower. This would grant them control over the pain and suffering they felt. When he reached this forest Siddhartha found five others already engaged in these practises. He impressed them with his determination and ability and before long they looked up to him, believing if any of them was to reach the final goal it would be him.

This path meant exposing himself to the outside world day and night, no matter what the weather. As time went on he ate less and less food and so began to wither away. Many accounts have it that he spent years in this kind of practise, becoming weaker as time went on. He was so weakened that at one point when he went to clean himself in the river he was almost pulled under by the current. It was then that he realised that this path had weakened him so much he could no longer even think clearly. What was the point of this when he couldn't even think straight afterwards. Siddhartha realised that he was now further from his goal than ever before and decided to end this dangerous and self destructive path. When the other ascetics saw him eating to regain strength they thought he must have abandoned his goal and left in disgust. They were bitterly disappointed by the leader they had so many hopes for, and even left the forest to continue their journey somewhere else.

Siddhartha regained the strength he needed to continue his journey and set of for another approach. This time he did not look for a teacher or established practise but decided to try one of his own that would have been developing in his mind for some time. The seekers of the Self and the ascetics had led assaults against the normal workings of the human mind and body. Siddhartha was beginning to wonder if it would not be better to work with the more positive aspects of our humanity rather than just fighting against the negative ones. What if, Siddhartha wondered, the path to overcome pain and suffering was built into us and didn't need to be forced upon us? Could it be possible that this state of liberation was built into the very structure of humanity?

Siddhartha remembered to when he was a child watching a plough make its way across a field. He saw worms and insects being pulled from the ground and cut to pieces by the working of the machinery and noticing the obvious pain and discomfort of the creatures he felt an overwhelming sense of compassion towards them. Suddenly because of what he was seeing and feeling he became blissful and lifted beyond his normal state of mind.

This kind of feeling is something most people have experienced at some point in their lives. This sense of being outside our normal selves can be provoked in many different ways. Sometimes a spectacular view or moving piece of art or music can touch us deeply and for a moment make us feel different or higher. Another common way of generating such experience is through the use of alcohol or drugs. The most obvious example of this case that can be linked to this kind of emotion is ecstasy. Users often note how their lack of egotism and selfishness under the influence gives them access to compassionate and blissful experiences beyond the ordinary. Within these moments we seem to leave our problems behind and inhabit a fuller version of ourselves.

Siddhartha decided to follow up on this kind of experience in his search for liberation. He crossed the river in the forest and found a comfortable place to continue this internal study beneath a fig tree. He had decided that the two extremes of luxury and deprivation were both equally damaging to humanity. Neither led to happiness and neither could help in finding the goal of overcoming pain and suffering. The true path had to be a middle way, between all extremes. This would be one of the central characteristics of the movement Siddhartha would found. It would always strike a middle ground between ways of living and philosophical positions. He remembered the state of mind that led to his experience of bliss as a child and decided to try and emulate the experience as best he could. Rather than attacking the ordinary workings of the mind he chose instead to do his best at amplifying the most positive and enjoyable workings of it. Already his practise would have given him the willpower and mental ability to be able to do this at a scale unimaginable to the untrained mind.

Siddhartha realised that the thing blocking these experiences from occurring was the human ego. It posited a self we all took for granted and strived for but which in actual fact prevented us from reaching any inner peace or happiness. It constantly tortures our minds with comparisons with others, negative emotions and unreasonable wants. The only reason people stuck with it was because they knew no other part of themselves to identify with. Siddhartha, however, discovered that whenever this ego is shaken or challenged, such as in feelings of great compassion, it releases a blissful energy that makes us feel complete and satisfied. Often those who encounter such feelings through drug induced experiences explain how the feeling of bliss is tied to them leaving their usual, mundane selves behind. Various religions have also made similar connections between true happiness and the abandonment of the ego. Christians, for example, speak about it in terms of self sacrifice, and how this brings us into the joyful presence of Jesus.

 As Siddhartha pressed on he began to understand just how superficial and problem causing the human ego really was. It constantly deluded itself and strived after ephemeral things while also seeking to control and dominate its environment, bringing misery both to itself and those around it. If fed it could grow to megalomaniacal dimensions and become highly destructive. People identified with it completely so followed its whims and selfish needs unaware that it was only a small part of their psychological makeup. The promises for the future it holds up usually came to nothing because of the deluded way in which it views the world. It is interesting that sociopaths are noted for the huge sense of self they harbour and how it blocks their view of other people's emotional states. For these kinds of people the world is only themselves. Most of the world's religions are aware of the nature of the human ego and are set up in large part as a method of combating its most destructive aspects. The lack of egotism and selfishness is one of the hallmarks of the truly religious. Even a moments respite from the constantly plotting and manipulating ego can bring immense benefits to its holder.

 Siddhartha began to see how he was to reach his final goal. The ego was formed as a deeply held and believed in sense of self that seemed to sit at the core of a person. It created a wall of separation by forming a barrier between that person and the rest of the world. People were deluded into believing that this self had an independent existence and was the crux of their personality. Siddhartha began to understand that this sense of self was an illusion that kept humanity back from its full potential. In many ways this was a radical departure from conventional thought. He agreed with his teachers in that there was no real conventional self but went further and said there was no real eternal Self either or even any kind of core self at all. Instead we were at one with the world around us and any sense of separation was a delusion. This sense of delusional separation was the main cause of our pain and suffering. He saw his experience as a child as being evidence of this to him. His compassion for the insects had broken down the wall of his self and exposed him to an immensely more fulfilling and richer way in which to exist. As these boundaries momentarily came down his small and self centred concerns revealed themselves for what they were and gave way to a greater sense of oneness with the world around him. Siddhartha now understood that the overcoming of pain and suffering meant the deliverance from our own self and immersion into this higher state of being.

As he sat beneath the fig tree we are told of what happened to Siddhartha towards the conclusion of his search. As in the story of his upbringing and renunciation it is best understood when told in its hagiographical format. It is described more technically in other texts, but not in any way someone outside of the movement Siddhartha would form would understand. To beginners and outsiders it is easiest understood hagiographicaly.

Siddhartha prepared himself at what is now known as the bodhi tree and vowed not to leave until he had reached this state of release from suffering. Mara was the name given to the god of darkness, delusion and selfishness in the local pantheon. In this account he is to be understood as the personification of all the delusion, doubt and egotism that plagued Siddhartha's mind, blocking him from his higher goal. In the story we hear how he had watched Siddhartha's journey with interest and had become increasingly worried as Siddhartha neared the end of his quest. He was aware that if the journey was completed his hold over the world would be deeply challenged. If Siddhartha were to win and then teach others how to achieve the same state of mind Mara would never be able to dominate humanity again. On the final night of the search Mara revealed himself to make a last fight against what was happening.

He began by unleashing his sons and daughters in waves of powerful and tempting delusions. Mara rose before Siddhartha in the form of a great Cakkavati, the position the soothsayers once foretold as a potential future of Siddhartha's. It was as if they were attempting to throw him of the path he was on by showing him what he could have become, what his father in actual fact wanted him to become. There is no doubt that this alternative life and position would have played on Siddhartha's mind. At the darkest moments of his journey he may have wondered what his life would have been like had he not left the palace but stayed to lead his people and make his father proud. What would his father thought if he saw his son starving himself, begging or spending hours in meditation rather than living in comfort and leading armies in glory as was once foretold. At this point, however, Mara's delusion had no effect on Siddhartha. He knew the importance of what he was doing now and how delusional the dreams of such a life were, so this had no effect on him or his efforts. This angered Mara, so he turned the army on Siddhartha to try and frighten him. Again this failed since Siddhartha realised the empty nature of what was before him.

Mara then unveiled his beautiful daughters who danced before him seductively. They offered Siddhartha themselves to try and distract him from his goal and remind him of the earthly pleasures that could be enjoyed. Again it had no effect on him, since he understood the utterly deluded nature of those who seek after such pleasures. No matter how beautiful or attractive they may seem the day will come when they will age and lose all of their physically attractive features. Even if they didn't, chasing after the fulfilment of such wants never leads to satisfaction of desire, only its amplification. Siddhartha remained indifferent to such attractions, knowing to abandon what he was about to achieve for such an empty thing would have been ridiculous.

Understanding that the lures of power and sex were having no effect Mara attempted an approach that struck closer to home. He made appear before Siddhartha's eyes the image of his wife and son, Yashodhara and Rahula. Mara probably counted on Siddhartha feeling guilty for leaving them behind without even saying goodbye to break his concentration. Now, the image seemed to suggest, isn't it time you went home to your wife and child who need you and dispensed with this silliness. Siddhartha, however, had already dealt with such doubts and knew that the best thing for his wife and son was to conquer Mara and teach them how to do the same.

Mara then stepped from the forest and approached Siddhartha to address him directly. He dismissed all of the delusions he had conjured and spoke quietly to his target. 'Who do you think you are', he asked 'to achieve where so many others have failed before you? What witnesses have you to confirm that you deserve what you seek after?' he mockingly asked. Here the attempt was now to make Siddhartha feel inferior and undeserving. He tried to convince him that he did not deserve to reach his goal and that even perhaps he was not capable of it. Instead Siddhartha reached forward with his right hand and touched the earth as his witness. The world had watched him in his journey and perceived the purely good intentioned nature of his quest. Since it was fact that he had struggled hard to uncover the true path to happiness Mara's attempts to plant the seeds of doubt had failed. The earth could only register the truth so it was Siddhartha's natural ally against Mara's lies and delusions. With this gesture Mara simply vanished, as if only a dream.

With all delusion and obstructions moved from his view Siddhartha spent the night delving deeper into his meditative state. As this went on his mind became increasingly luminous and capable of dealing with subtler levels of ignorance and mistaken beliefs until his mind became entirely cleansed of all but joy and wisdom. The walls separating him from the world were brought down completely and his ego would never get in the way of his enjoyment of life ever again. By the time morning came he had reached his full potential, therefore becoming fully awakened to himself and his relationship to the world around him. He described this state of mind as nirvana, a term referring to the snuffing out of his ego. It is important to remember that he did not annihilate this part of his mind but revealed it for the delusion it always was. He had become, as was foretold by the soothsayer at his birth, a Buddha.

It is unlikely Siddhartha achieved this state after one night but rather that it took a much longer and more drawn out effort. He later described the gradual withdrawing of the mundane mind and the revealing of the Buddha mind as a process, like a sword being slowly withdrawn from its scabbard. It meant the creation of an entirely different kind of being free from selfishness, egotism and misery. As the Buddha would also say 'the scabbard was one thing, the sword something entirely different'. The religious scholar Karen Armstrong has put forward an interesting hypothesis to try and explain this kind of change. She mentions that it may be possible that because evolutionary development has caused our minds to develop in such a way as to benefit our own survival only, that when this is challenged by emotions such as compassion it unleashes an entirely different mode of consciousness altogether. There is no doubt that this other mode is entirely different to our day to day experience.

Mara is useful in this story in illustrating how difficult the process is and the level of resistance that the ego can put up to fight for its survival. This internal dictator does not lie down quietly to die but will fight against the better interests of its host for control. It is rooted so deeply in us that a challenge to it often feels like a challenge to our deepest identity.

The Buddha would have been in his mid thirties when he achieved this state of nirvana. All traditions agree that he lived to around the age of eighty which would have meant his teaching mission lasted around forty five years. At first he spent some time by himself in the forest considering and enjoying his achievement. It would seem as if he was reluctant to go out and teach because of concerns that others would not understand his dharma. He knew he would be misunderstood and was sceptical of other people's ability or desire to achieve what he had done. He knew how deeply many cherished and even depended upon the self. Not only would he be telling them to abandon it but that it was an illusion and never really existed at all. Eventually he decided that although many would not understand or heed his message there were some who would, and for their sake he would go out and teach his dharma.

At first he wanted to teach his old masters, Alara Kalama and Uddaka Ramapatta, but he heard word that they had recently died. He was saddened that they had missed out on the chance of being taught the path to true happiness but continued on anyway. Next he decided to find the five ascetics he had left just prior to discovering his own dharma. He found them in a deer park, near the holy city of Benares continuing with their search and approached them. When they saw the Buddha coming they remembered him as giving up on his journey and did not welcome him. It was only as he came closer to them that they knew something different had come over him. He was no longer the same as when he left. They offered him a seat amongst them and asked him to reveal what had caused this obvious change in him. The Buddha then delivered his first teaching. This is referred to as turning the wheel of the dharma, in reference to the movement of knowledge from him to those around him. As he spoke the ascetics understood all that he said and found it agreed with their own experience. They had followed a similar trajectory as he had so were particularly ripe for the teachings. They adopted his system and found that they too experienced the same results he did. The Buddha would find that his teachings were received with great relief among other spiritual practitioners. At last their search for the eternal Self could end in the realisation that no such thing existed. The burden of constantly searching for this was now lifted from them.

When research was being carried out during the 19th century on the Buddha's teachings some of the titles given to its elements were translated in a way that blurs their true meaning. Even the title given by the West to the movement misunderstands its very nature. The term 'Buddhism' seems to categorise it as some kind of ideology or rigid thought system when in a very real way the Buddha's teachings are the antithesis to all ideology and -ism's. A more accurate name for the teachings is that of the Buddha-Dharma. Just as the term Mohammedans was relinquished because of the incorrect nature of Islam it portrayed, perhaps the term Buddhism will fall out of use as more accurate understanding of it spread. For now, however, since this is the term most people understand the Buddha's following as I will continue to use it at times.

Within the teachings terms such as *The Four Noble Truths* have been placed on parts, which as well as sounding slightly presumptuous, can make hazy the true meaning of the term. The nobility about these truths, according to the Buddha, was in the person who understands them. This ties in with the Buddha's revolutionary conceptions of what it was that created true nobility in a person. In a society so dominated by birth status as the true sign of human worth, the Buddha's message that nirvana was open to all shook it at its foundations. As the merchants rose and the old castes began to lose meaning his message found new recruits who were attracted to the idea of teachings that could be adopted by any caste. It did not matter who you were born to, nobility was only to be acquired by your behaviour and actions. A new kind of Brahmin was being formed that did not depend upon their parent's birth status. *The Noble Eightfold Path* is another such title. Again the nobility is in those who follow.

In the deer park the Buddha began his teachings by outlining the *Four Noble Truths* for the five ascetics. In an oral culture knowledge and information would have been preserved in formats such as this in order to make it easier to remember. The Buddha's time alone before going out to teach would have been spent re-tracing the process he had gone through to reach nirvana and breaking it down into a method easy to remember.

The First Noble Truth is that life is *dukkha*. This term is normally translated into English as life is suffering, thereby giving rise to the old accusations of the Buddha-Dharma being pessimistic or fatalist. It would be more accurate to understand it as saying that life contains suffering, which includes physical pain and mental anguish. It is not pessimistic to make this assertion, but rather realistic. Life does contain suffering and anyone who denies this is deluded. The word *dukkha* is better translated as un-satisfactoriness. It feels as if life is lacking in something, or that it is not what it was supposed to be. We often imagine ourselves fulfilling goals and feeling complete but never actually get there. It as if in some way life is awry or has lost its way but we still have intimations of some other, better way of being that we never seem able to reach.

The Second Noble Truth is concerned with what the Buddha held responsible for this sense of un-satisfactoriness. It was the greedy and insatiable self at the core of human beings. He described it as craving, as in the self's craving to dominate and hold onto the world around it. *Dukkha* was caused by our craving for control or objects of security and status from the world around us. The ego cannot stop trying to ensure its own perpetual survival, which being impossible, meant it go's on craving forever. Craving leads to attachment to things in the world around us that we think give us security or pleasurable sensual experience. We are also attached to our views and ideas about the world around us because they form another security barrier against the unpredictable world beyond them. This is the way in which the ideologies of the 19th and 20th centuries provided comfort to their adherents. When these attachments are challenged it is another cause of suffering, as we do not like to be separated from what gives us comfort. These cravings, the Buddha taught, were incompatible with the true nature of reality. All things are impermanent so craving after something only meant chasing after illusions and things that would change or disappear in time. This gives rise to a constant sense of frustration that becomes painful when constantly reinforced.

Craving after things also meant that the illusion of the self is constantly strengthened. This feeling of want only broadens the distance felt between the self and the world around us because of the distance between ourselves and what we desire. The delusions of craving and the delusions of the self were deeply intertwined and made one another grow stronger. Liberation from suffering, the Buddha taught, was to be found in release from this constant neediness and the misconceptions it forms and the relaxation of the ego that this would bring.

The Third Noble Truth is that there is a way of escaping this network of delusion and suffering. More specifically there is a way of being that is beyond the reach of all these false beliefs and their inherent sorrow and that this is what the Buddha called nirvana. It is a way of releasing all the forces that power these illusions and frees the mind from greed, hatred and delusion. Samsara was the name given by the Buddha to the conventional and deluded way in which the mind perceived the world. The three marks of samsara are dissatisfaction, impermanence and no-inherent existence. Relief from this condition can only be found in nirvana.

The Buddha-Dharma therefore is the road that leads from samsara to nirvana. For the Buddha, though, nirvana was not only a choice or one possible option for humanity to pursue, but something all people sought after whether they were aware of it or not. It was built into the very structure of humanity and the world around it. In one form or another we will always seek for this release from the limits of our ego and immersion in something greater. Drug use, sex, art and ideology all give us intimations of something higher than ourselves. It is our interactions with this layer of reality that provides all of the meaning and joy in our lives. Even other religions attempt to provide this experience to its adherents but describes it in other terms, such as being in the presence of God for Christians, immersion in Brahman for Hindi's or intimations of Zion in Rastafarianism. Whether through the use of ecstasy or Christian prayer this kind of experience always couples a release of the self and the encountering of a higher reality and is as natural to humanity as sex or hunger. This search, so often found in the form of religion, was not some external system imposed upon human beings but manifested from within them. Those who avoid or shun such experience often find that their lives become barren and empty, without motivation or colour. In all of these forms the experience is often short lived but is still highly effective. Nirvana was the term given by the Buddha to our final immersion into this life enhancing state.

 The Fourth Noble Truth concerned the path the Buddha had drawn out for us as most conducive to encounter and eventually rest in this state of mind. It, in typical embarrassingly translated form, is known as the *Noble Eightfold Path*. It would be better to understand it as an eight dimensioned path since each of its factors were to be practised simultaneously, rather than in any particular order. The eight factors of the path are split under three headings; wisdom, morality and meditation.

 Under wisdom we should adopt the most appropriate views and intentions as to bring us to the realisations the Buddha made. Concerning the most correct view, he means for us to live in conformity to reality and to the world around us. It was believing in things that were contradictory to reality that ended up bringing about suffering. In this sense ignorance is not bliss, but rather the cause of pain and anguish. When deeply held views that are wrong are challenged or proven incorrect the effect can often be devastating on an individual. Look at the way Europeans reacted to the way in which new scientific discoveries challenged their religious views. Or even how former dissenters from these views were treated in Christian societies. Our views should have some basis in experience or what we have learned from the world around us. The Buddha was entirely empirical in his approach and encouraged others to be the same. He would not have taught about nirvana or the path to it unless he had experience of it himself. In a more philosophical sense having the appropriate view meant having no views at all. It was true that a person could be relatively more correct or accurate in their thinking than another but ultimately we are all wrong. No view ever corresponds perfectly with reality but is always mistaken in some way or other. This is the main mistake of the secular ideologies. They created a description of the world that became a set of views that people took as a complete description of reality. These views were laid out like a blanket over the world, blocking the individual's ability to see what was really there. Communists and Nazi's could not really see what they were creating because their opinions and understandings of the world were blocking the way. This meant that we should not hold on to any of our opinions absolutely since one way or another reality would contradict them. How we thought the world worked was not how it worked so we should never mistake it for such. Our understandings can only ever be provisional. Again this an example of how the purely logical, rational parts of the mind were limited and how certain realms of knowledge went beyond them.

Appropriate intentions meant the motivation behind our search for nirvana. It had to be free of all egotism and motivated by benevolent causes. If it were any different then it would be impossible to reach nirvana. Many would have approached the Buddha-Dharma with the aim of enhancing the self rather than escaping it. Aware of it or not they imagine themselves acquiring fame or being admired and worshipped by others because of their spiritual achievements. For people such as this nirvana would always be out of reach. Right intention also meant being strongly enough motivated for the right reasons as well. This task was not an easy one and would require a strong basis to push it forward. It also meant abandoning anything that could lead to the ego's selfish habit of attachment. As mentioned before attachment is incompatible with the nature of reality.

The Sword From The Scabbard

The effect abandoning attachment in life was subtle but immensely powerful. It was not required for a practitioner to give everything up, but only their attachment to it.

Morality covered the practitioner's speech, action and livelihood in their day to day lives. In reference to speech, it meant to refrain from talking hurtfully, falsely or idly but rather encouragingly and beneficially. In terms of action it meant avoiding behaviour that could be counted as sexual misconduct, harmful to others or theft of property. For livelihood it meant not any job or activity that infringed upon appropriate speech or action. All of these precepts were designed to counter the ego's control over the life of the practitioner and lead them to another way of perceiving the world. They are similar to many of the commandments and rules of other religions except that instead of being dictated from above they were for the practitioner's own good. The self caused people to lie and hurt others for its own gain, unaware and uncaring of the effects this behaviour has upon the world. As well as the suffering that occurs naturally in life the self added to it for its own gain. The Buddha's program was designed to show not only that the self was an illusion, but that it was possible to live without it. By not reacting to the self's every whim and want people could gradually free themselves of its control.

The wisdom and morality dimensions help the adherent in what could be counted as the most important aspect of the Buddha-Dharma, the meditative dimension. In the yoga that was used at this time in India, a basic training in morality and ethics was a prerequisite for the learning of yogic practises and advanced meditation. The untapped abilities these practises could bring out made the learners mind much more powerful and able than the average persons. So much so that they could be highly dangerous if they had no kind of ethical grounding. For the Buddha-Dharma meditation was to be the tool with which the truths the Buddha taught could be revealed to his followers. They will see through its use that the self does not exist, but is rather a perpetually moving set of mental states without any inherent existence. Then they will gain control over these states and be able to change and alter them at will, preventing the manifestation of negative ones and encouraging the rise of positive ones. The centrality of awareness in this meditative state would enable the individual to become conscious of the way in which his mind worked and eventually be able to trace how and why such states of mind are created. This would all require appropriate amounts of effort, mindfulness and concentration. Meditation will increase the practitioners will power and give them more control over their minds than they ever thought possible. It would also uncover unresolved or difficult issues that alter their day to day behaviour that could prove beneficial to their overcoming of suffering. Meditation also meant an end to the constant moving and chasing that animates so many lives. The mind would finally rest from these endless concerns and often to its surprise discover what it was running from.

Only the desperately disturbed cannot meditate but there are few who do not find it difficult at first. This is evidence of just how restless the mind truly is. Even in sleep it is constantly turning and working as we know from our dreams. In meditative states it is finally at rest and can deal with itself. The benefits of meditative practise are well documented and, once getting over the initial embarrassment of attempting it, people have discovered how it can greatly enrich life. Meditation causes the mind to slow down enough to see how things really are and how it really works. By doing so it allows us to work through all of the blocks of delusion that stand in the way of attaining nirvana. By meditating on the causes of hatred and greed it would become increasingly easy to overcome and counter them. The Buddha also taught his followers to practise the Four Immeasurables when in a meditative state. We are to develop *metta*; an all pervading and non discriminatory friendliness and compassion for those in the world around us. *Karuna* is a happiness and delight in the gains and happiness of others. *Mudita* is a total equanimity towards all of the different people in our lives. What these three practises bring to the adherent was a loosening of the ego's centralised place in their worldview. All of the emotions attached to them weakened the walls that the self had built around itself to be insulated from the outside world. The practise of compassion is a virtue emphasised in all of the world's religions because of the extraordinary benefits it can bring upon the practitioner and those around them. The Buddha did not mean it in the sappy or emotionally indulgent way that fills modern soaps or dramatic film but as a clear and disciplined application. It has long been noticed how compassion and its associated emotions are able to open up area's of our humanity that would otherwise be closed of to us. The fourth immeasurable is *upekkha* and is concerned with deeper levels of meditation and concentration known as the *jhanas*. It is at the fourth *jhana* that above ordinary experiences and abilities are to be found. Eventually we would come to see how the Buddha saw the world, not as a thing that exists but as a process, a constant flow and change with us in it.

As mentioned so much so far, the central liberating truth of the Buddha's message is that there is no self. If something were this self that we believed in and protected so much then it would obey what we want and not be so difficult to predict or control. When we thought about it even at the most basic level, we could not say that either the mental or the physical was this self. All that comes together to create us is, under inspection, not us. Following this all that creates us is non self. We are better understood as impermanent and casually created psychophysical bundles. The self we all believe in is a fiction and utterly unsubstantial. We throw a consistent personality upon something which is entirely not, and become upset and confused when it is challenged. Persons are no more than easy reference points for bundles of energy that have happened to come together. This aspect of the Buddha-Dharma has been found disturbing and frightening by many and led to accusations of nihilism from other schools of thought. On closer analysis, however, it is discovered that the relinquishing of the self gives room to something much greater. This delusion of personality does little more than lock us within certain patterns of thought and action that keeps us unaware of the potential for change that exists behind it.

Another central feature of the Buddha-Dharma is Dependent Origination. Everything is locked into a relationship of cause and effect with the world around it. Most importantly, our consciousness depends on reaction to the world around it to exist. An example is our visual consciousness, which can only exist when there is something provoking it, thereby causing us to see. Consciousness is the flow of these cause and effects and the experiences they give rise to when they occur. This system of thought renders divine forces and creators irrelevant. Everything that exists is the result of countless causes and effects so nothing can exist independently or spontaneously. This is the main argument to be found in the Buddha's teachings against the existence of a creator God. This dependence of each on all other things means that in a constantly changing universe nothing can remain still and isolated. Impermanence is one of realities deepest and most primary features. All is so deeply interconnected that seemingly unconnected events and beings are actually tied to each other at a fundamental level. This Dependent Origination is essential in the Buddha-Dharma because it links suffering with certain causes, that if removed can bring the practitioner to happiness and internal peace. If suffering were caused by some supernatural source or divine interventionist it would not be possible to overcome it. We would not be able to rely on the cause and effects that bring about nirvana to be confident enough to attempt it. Dependent Origination also helped explain one of the phenomenon's the Buddha discovered affecting human existence in particular.

Reincarnation had grown at this time to become a commonly held belief to what happens to a person after death. Although some schools maintained annihilation after death, the growing belief in an eternal Self had left many to wonder what happened to it after the death of the body. Most schools came to understand reincarnation as this eternal Self moving from the dead being to create and animate the existence of a new life. This belief frightened many when they considered being reborn somewhere else, into another life containing pain and suffering. The Buddha came to a different understanding of what happened after death. There was no eternal Self but the consciousness that underlined human experience did not annihilate with the death of the body. Nothing in the universe could simply disappear out of existence in this way. Just like the other parts of the human being it was made of a specific form of energy that did not disappear with death. As the body returns to the earth at death, consciousness also moves on but changes form. The habitual patterns it has gathered in the former life helps shape the nature of this new existence. The Buddha did not think of the person in this other life as being the same as this one, but rather being dependent on the previous person's existence and merely using the same chain of mental energy. It would be a false belief to think of this person as oneself, especially considering the Buddha's message that nothing even in this life constitutes a self. This creation of new lives by the residual consciousness of the old was motivated by the deep seeded cravings left over by the previous personality. This was why upon reaching nirvana the chain would stop, and consciousness would rest in an indescribable state known as parinirvana.

As the Buddha taught all of this the five ascetics realised his teachings importance and became the first members of the Buddha's sangha. The word sangha can be understood as a union, and most teachers at this time had their own. As word spread of the effectiveness of his teachings more people joined his union and his fame spread. It is recorded that crowds would come out to see this Buddha when he approached their towns and cities. As was to be expected other teachers became annoyed about this and publicly challenged his doctrines and teachings. It surprised them that he was able to handle this kind of criticism with ease and even convince them of the rightness of his views. Many of these teachers and their students joined his union when they discovered that he had laid out the correct path.

There is a story told of how the Buddha handled metaphysical speculation and world views. A student came to him and said he would join the union if he could have asked questions concerning the nature of reality answered. His questions are interesting in that they are ones that still provoke heated debate today. He asked questions such as whether the world was infinite or not, whether there existed a God or not, whether the Buddha existed after death and so on. Throughout this entire session the Buddha remained completely silent until his interviewer left. He explained afterwards to his other followers that he could not answer the mans questions without implanting false beliefs in him. If he were to confirm the existence of a God he would only be confirming that mans conceptions of what God was to him. The same went for all of the other questions. Not only were they unanswerable to the conceptual mind but the questions themselves were in a large way inadequate. He explained that it was if the man asking such questions was shot by a poisoned arrow but refused the cure until certain answers about the source, type and potency of the poison were answered. Suffering was the poison, nirvana the cure. Becoming lost in unanswerable questions was pointless.

Another story was the metaphor of the raft. The Buddha described humanity as inhabiting one shore of a river called samsara. At the other shore of the river was nirvana. Whilst most people wasted their lives running up and down this shore his dharma was a raft that would carry people across the river. The point of the metaphor was that when one reached the other shore the raft must be left behind since it would only be a burden. The Buddha's teachings were not to be clinged to in such a way but left behind when the other shore is reached. They were purely provisional and attachment to them would be entirely counter productive. This attitude helps explain the Buddha-Dharma's ability to adapt itself to various cultures and places throughout history. More importantly it prevents the emergence of any kind of fundamentalist strain from ever emerging. The Buddha-Dharma could never be considered absolute in the way some other religions have come to view their teachings.

Within the Buddha's own lifetime the union he founded numbered in the tens of thousands. It came to be a force to be reckoned with in the Gangetic Plains and it even became a concern at one point that too many people were joining to be able to handle. Today the movement numbers in the hundreds of millions and all can trace themselves and their teachings back to the Buddha. It can be found in every inhabited continent and has made an indelible impact on human history. It was not a religion, in our sense of the word, he believed he was founding, since he would not have been familiar with such a concept. As mentioned it is recorded that he only expected the following to last a few hundred years at most. He accepted that in time the wheel would stop turning and what he had discovered would be forgotten, but believed it possible that some day in the future someone else would rediscover it and begin teaching it again. He maintained that he had not invented the path, but merely rediscovered it. That humanity, at various times and places, had known and understood these teachings but that they had become clouded or lost as time went on. All religions and followings had at their core this path but it had overgrown with weeds and plants. All he had done was cut the path clear revealing it to those around him. In time, though, he knew and even expected that the path would become obscure again.

 As he promised the Buddha returned to his place of birth to see those he had left years before. When he got there, realising what he had achieved, his wife and child forgave him for leaving in the manner he did. Here he found many new followers including his father Suddhodana. Proud that his son was now the Buddha and leader of thousands Suddhodana also forgave him for disobeying him years before. It was around then that the Buddha began to ordain women followers, something utterly unheard of at this place and point in time. He knew the controversy that it would cause and was reluctant to do so at first. Not only was he flouting the caste system but now he was ordaining women into his union. It was the aunt who raised him who convinced him to do so and so she became its first female member. King Bimbisara of Magadha, followed by a large number of his subjects, became a lay follower of the Buddha causing the Buddha's union to suddenly jump in size.

 Time went on and the Buddha grew older, constantly teaching and accepting new followers, who came to be referred to as stream-enterers. As he reached old age he seemed to increasingly avoid the busy cities and towns in exchange for solitude and more secluded places. He travelled most places with a faithful friend and servant called Nalanda. When the Buddha was around the age of 80 he and Nalanda stopped at the village of Kushinagar. The Buddha lay down here and announced that his time had come and he was to pass away soon. Nalanda was annoyed his teacher would die in this abandoned place but the Buddha explained how this place was once busy and joyful. Now it was deserted, as all places will be some day. With many of his followers gathered around him he reminded them of some of the core principles he taught; that all things are impermanent and to work out their salvation with diligence. Entering deeper states of meditation the Buddha died calmly, apparently on the anniversary of his attainment of nirvana over forty years earlier. Some of his followers were devastated but those who understood his teachings deepest were peaceful in the face of his death, understanding that his consciousness could now rest in parinirvana without his body holding it back any longer.

The Sword From The Scabbard

He left no successor to lead the movement, as was common practise at this time, because he saw his dharma as manifesting the leadership people should follow. He told his followers that to see him all they had to do was look at the Buddha-Dharma, for he was it and it was him. He seemed to have been afraid of a personality cult developing around him that would take away from the individuals own search for nirvana. By idolising him and his achievement they would be putting such achievement for themselves beyond reach. He would have been pleased by the way in which those who follow the Buddha-Dharma today are able to make this distinction and do not think of him as superhuman or godlike. One famous statement from a teacher indicated that if you meet the Buddha, kill the Buddha. Our concepts and ideas about him must not get in the way of us reaching nirvana. It could be seen that upon attaining nirvana he became more identified with this higher reality but this, as he always taught, was a possibility open to all of us. Those outside the Buddha-Dharma often assume that the Buddha is considered some kind of deity or idol by his followers. In fact he was absorbed into India's Hindu pantheon as a manifestation of a certain god but at this time his teachings had already spread to other parts of the world where a more accurate version of them were preserved.

Statues of the Buddha began to be made hundreds of years after his death to remind practitioners what lay inside themselves and as a representation of his dharma. The first artistic representations of him were made years before and were created only as footprints left in the ground. A clever representation of his lack of self and the non existence of his ego.

The Buddha's teachings define most clearly all of the answers to humanities problems that the Axial Age produced. Judaism, as we now know it, was formed along with its emphasis on good treatment of the poor and the sick. Humanity through such acts could commune with a higher way of being, which they understood as being in God's presence. This would go on to influence Christianity and Islam's understanding of being with God as only possible through overcoming our selfishness and egotism. In many cases some have attempted to equate nirvana with God. Where practitioners dislike this is in that God is too limited a concept to describe nirvana. The Buddha's teachings would even go on to change the religious customs he was born into and help shape what we now know as Hinduism. In China Taoism perceived the universe to be infused with an ineffable force known as the Tao. This Tao could only be touched upon by humanity when all else but the present moment was forgotten. Although most of these movements began with these motives at their heart, in time they would be forgotten or lost to be replaced by metaphysical belief systems or rules that have lost all meaning.

His teachings made the idea of reliance by the mind to anything outside of it ridiculous. In a world characterised only by its impermanent and transitory nature this was essential to survive and flourish. There are no beliefs or structures that cannot be challenged or destroyed and to believe in some as such is ridiculous.

For the Buddha human egotism was the source of the world's problems and human suffering. Unlike many other followings evil was not something external from humanity but something to be rooted out from within it. The primary focus of this task is upon the mind. Since it filters the world we see around us altering it meant altering that world. We would come to see, through quieting the mind, how it really works, and how much of the world is our own projection. The world has always been seen not as it is, but as we are. Although it is certainly true that our moods alter how we perceive the world the Buddha would have went further than this and said that how our minds work forms the world we see.

As psychologically astute as the Buddha was it is likely he understood the received deities and gods as projections of human needs and desires. Even if he did believe in some form of gods or goddess' he certainly considered them useless. It was up to humanity to make its own way and find its own answers rather than wait for divine intervention. His understanding of reality being controlled by laws of cause and effect foreshadows modern science and how we view the world today. For him to come to this understanding independently is quite an achievement in itself.

Misconceptions continue to exist about the nature of the Buddha and his teachings. Some will always imagine at the sound of his name a fat, Japanese man or that his followers are all vegetarians or pacifists. Or as one friend of mine did when hearing the word Buddhism, strike a pose of a Hindu deity and say 'Om'. In this way it is assumed that it is only valid for some cultures and untranslatable elsewhere. Others think of reincarnation and are immediately put of by the idea of it. They associate metaphysical beliefs they consider ridiculous to the centre of the practise and automatically consider it invalid. How could the Buddha's teachings have anything to tell us when he believed in something so obviously wrong? If the Buddha had been questioned on anything like this he would have explained to the inquirer how such small things like beliefs do not even matter. What is important is the here and now and the experiences beliefs are there to give rise to.

 Others still misunderstand and see it as pessimistic or nihilistic, choosing escape from the world in its ethos of renunciation. One book, written in the 19th century explained how if reincarnation did not exist then the Buddhist answer to existence is suicide. Ideas such as this continue to influence how some view the Buddha-Dharma. Even today some accuse it of seeking to annihilate the human personality or having an entirely negative world view. This can be easily responded to when considering the highly sociable nature of Buddhist monks or that the Buddha's explanation that the world is good but we need to change to be able to truly see it.

 Others even will look at the Buddha-Dharma and decide that there may have been something in it but it is not applicable to people living in the world today. Or that our modern methods of deriving knowledge are superior and cannot be reconciled with it. Is there really room in modern psychotherapy or neural science for something like nirvana? Is it really possible to overcome suffering in this way? Taking time out to alter how we think isn't really going to help prevent war and disease, is it? Some would reckon that the Buddha may have made a mistake and overemphasised the importance of the mind over the world. Is it possible, as in so many other movements, that he and his followers were simply deluded? Hasn't the West's success been due to its focus on manipulating the external world? Previous scientific discoveries and descriptions of reality do appear to counter the Buddha's understanding of reality and its relation to the mind. If consciousness is the result only of the workings of the brain then his conceptions of it are very different from scientific understandings. If rebirth does not exist then the search to escape suffering is not as fervent as it was when he was alive, since it's going to end with death anyway. Or why waste time following a *Noble Eightfold Path* if we have only a short time to live. It may eventually lead to real happiness but it is not an easy path to follow and many of the so called pleasurable experiences we encounter are reduced by it. With the Buddha's respect for truth and empirical evidence it would be wrong to accept any of his teachings if evidence appeared to contradict it. If all of it was true then there should be some evidence of it or at the very least no evidence directly contradicting it.

The Sword From The Scabbard

PART THREE

The Sword From The Scabbard

5

The borders of science

It is inadvisable to attach any kind of religious or guiding belief to scientific discovery. The nature of scientific answers and explanations is that they are usually only provisional understandings accepted until more evidence comes to light to explain something clearer. One example of this kind of change in scientific understanding is that of gravity; our current understandings of it as curves in space and time differ greatly from the commonly understood force sucking from the centre of the earth. Those who equate events such as the Big Bang with the creation accounted for in Genesis are only picking and choosing parts from scientific research. There is much more to contradict the creation account of Genesis in the annals of scientific discovery than there is to encourage belief in it. Of course no one can say with absolute certainty, as of yet, that the world wasn't created by some divine being, but there is no reason why it should have to be God as understood by Christianity. Bertrand Russell once remarked he would find it easier to agree with the Gnostics and conclude some kind of demon formed the world. Even in philosophical circles some jump on scientific discovery in this way. Proponents of free will once held up the discoveries of the quantum revolution as evidence that the world was not deterministic.

The Sword From The Scabbard

Belief systems such as Christianity and Islam should be better understood as art forms outside the realm of scientific analysis. Genesis or God, for Christians, should not need scientific evidence but understood internally as pointers to a reality beyond scientific reach. The Buddha-Dharma, however, could be considered differently in some ways. It's philosophical and life focused nature means that it can be justified to probe it with scientific research. The Buddha's emphasis on empirical research and his come and see attitude displays a high level of confidence about his teachings, and even makes it feel as if he would have relished the research that it is now possible to do upon them.

The Buddha held up a promise that his teachings could deliver us from pain and suffering. The best question of them that can be asked is if this is true. Scientific research needs an entirely objective nature for it to be considered valid. Simply asking a practitioner of the Buddha-Dharma whether they are happier may be interesting but it cannot satisfy a truly scientific interest. The entirely subjective nature of something like happiness also makes it impossible to measure objectively. There is no way of knowing for certain if they are telling the truth or if they happened to be born with a happier disposition than most people but mistakenly attribute it to the Buddha. Or that they are deluded in some deeper way. Luckily for those interested it has, in recent times, become possible to probe these areas in an interesting and scientifically legitimate manner.

Mattieu Ricard is a great example of the way in which the Buddha's teachings can reach into and affect our lives here in the modern West. He was raised in France and is the son of a highly distinguished philosopher and writer called Jean-Francois Revel. Revel's books have covered topics such as religion and ideology and include titles such as *Without Marx or Jesus* and *The Totalitarian Temptation*. Ricard grew up surrounded by the elite of French intellectual life and eventually began a promising career in the area of cellular genetics. While at university he viewed footage a friend of his had taken of Buddhist monks escaping the Chinese occupation of Tibet. He was immediately taken in by the footage and developed an interest. When he travelled to meet some of these practitioners he was impressed by their demeanour and way of life. He decided after finishing his degree to join them and is now living as a practitioner of the Buddha-

Dharma and working on humanitarian projects in Tibet and Nepal. What is so interesting about his choice of this life is his upbringing and how well versed he would have been in scientific analysis and Western philosophy. It is interesting that someone educated in cellular genetics had no problem accepting the Buddha's teachings and reconciling it with what he has learned.

Ricard has taken part recently in the *Mind and Life Meetings*, a series of organised meetings between top scientists and Buddhist leaders. One of their most interesting area's of discussion and research is concerned with the method with which the physical brain structures itself. Twenty years ago it was assumed that the brain was solid and that after development in youth, other than examples of brain damage, would not change until degeneration in old age sets in. Today we know about something called neuroplasticity. This refers to how the physical brain is constantly evolving in response to experience through creating new or strengthening already existing connections between neurons. What this means is that change in the mind is not only possible but that it can be reflected in changes in the very structure of the physical brain.

For those who claim that no real change can be made to how an individual thinks or acts this is evidence to the contrary. However, it does contradict changes that are supposed to occur overnight or instantaneously. Such changes usually are short lived and superficial anyway. Changes in thought patterns takes long term effort and practise to form. The changes the Buddha encouraged us to make in ourselves takes long term effort utterly unlike the concept of an instant conversion. To be suddenly born again is probably something that suit's the modern day ethos of instant gratification but the Buddha's advice is not something that could be considered a quick fix answer. The changes he sought to bring about are more gradual but reach much deeper. It could be compared to a musician being trained to use an instrument over a number of years. No one expects them to be instantly good or even capable but over time their ability increases as their brains are able to form new connections and strengthen already existing useful ones to this activity. An example of the results of neural plasticity is the higher level of activity that can be detected in the parts of the brain dealing with musical ability in accomplished musicians. Another study on London taxi drivers has found a larger part of their brains are devoted to dealing with maps and directions. What neuroplasticity explains is how we become better at an activity with practise and experience.

Richard Davidson of the W.M. Keck Laboratory set out to see what effect, if any, meditation would have upon the physical brain and if it could in any way alter its shape. In November of 2004 the Proceedings of the National Academy of Sciences published papers of the effects of long term meditation. For practitioners of the Buddha-Dharma meditation is the central practise of the path. Any changes practitioners report on their thought patterns would gain great credibility if it could be supported by evidence of change in the behaviour of the physical brain.

There are mainly two ways of testing mental states and brain activity. Electroencephalogram (EEG) records changes in the brains electrical activity responding to which area's of the brain are active. Functional magnetic resonance imaging (FMRI) measures the blood flow through areas of the brain providing the precise location of cerebral activity.

Tests done during meditation reveal an increase in the amount of gamma brain waves that are detected. These brain waves appear to better organised, displaying a greater level of coordination and synchronicity, than normal brainwaves. What this confirms is that meditation can reach areas of our conscious spectrum normally closed to us. Enough meditative practises even seem to give the practitioner some ability to deliberately regulate cerebral activity. The longer the participant practised meditation the more concentrated were the levels of gamma waves. This shows that meditation does indeed alter the way physical aspects of the brain operate. It would appear that not only are mediators feeling the changes they report but that the physical activity of the brain reflects these changes. The importance of these discoveries is it that they show the Buddha to be correct in teaching that the mind and how we think can be trained and modified.

The physical brain has no emotional centre or anything that would correspond to any kind of central processor. Each sensation we feel and chain of thought we follow works through the interaction and co-operation of several regions of it. It has been noticed, however, that there is an increased level of activity in the left prefrontal cortex when the subject is experiencing positive emotions and mental states. Reflecting this, negative emotional states have also been associated with the right prefrontal cortex. Relations between these two areas of the brain vary from person to person but does reflect quite accurately individual temperament. Those more prone to a gloomy world view or depression have shown more activity in the right hemisphere and those with a more positive outlook show increased activity in the left hemisphere. It may seem simplistic but more activity on the left does indicate the predominance of pleasant feelings. Those who raise up and focus on positive mental states during meditation, as the Buddha taught, have been able to shift this balance more to the left, indicating increased levels of happiness and contentment. When they meditate upon compassionate feelings an especially large increase in activity is recorded in the left prefrontal cortex. It has been even noticed at times to almost overcome all activity in the right prefrontal cortex. It would appear that there is something very real in the Buddha's connection of compassion towards others with the overcoming of inner suffering. Becoming compassionate towards others does indeed create a stronger form of happiness within us.

Certain emotions provoke small flickers of muscle movement on our faces that are often difficult to pick up. If someone is attempting to avoid displaying a certain emotion these small movements normally still cannot be suppressed. They are so hard to notice, however, that they are referred to as microexpressions. They will always correspond to what we are really feeling and cannot be easily faked. During tests those experienced in meditation have shown themselves able to pick up on these microexpressions better than any other tested group, including policemen, lawyers, psychiatrists, customs officials and judges.

Another ability those who meditate are capable of is the suppression of what is known as the startle reflex. This is what makes us jump when we hear a loud noise or see a frightening image. It would seem that what causes this reflex is being sucked into the present moment so suddenly by something which shocks us. Meditation, however, teaches us to inhabit the present moment entirely, so no shock is needed to pull us into the present.

The experience of the self losing its hold over people entirely, described as nirvana, cannot be held in the same category as the discoveries of these experiments. Yes, the Buddha's path does appear to make people happier and more content, as the changes in the left prefrontal cortex's activity has shown. This happiness has been linked with the deliberate manifestation of positive states of mind that oppose the sense of self inherent in all of us. It is also true, however, that becoming more aware of the present moment or feeling happier through loosening this sense of self is still some distance away from experiencing an entire absence of the self. Can this kind of research give us any indication that such an experience is even possible? Andrew Newberg, a neuroscientist, seems to have discovered evidence to affirm this. Towards the rear of the physical brain are what is known as the parietal lobes. They have been described as the brain's orientation association areas and seem to control the limits of what we define as our selves. Newberg's work on those undergoing deep states of meditation has shown that some practitioners are able to cut off this area of the brain thereby inducing what they describe as mystical states. The boundaries formed by the parietal lobes disappear and along with it the limited sense of a self. Now they feel themselves expanded as the border between themselves and the rest of the world comes down. When the self is shut down the experience is always described as a merging with something greater rather than non existence. In all cases it is described in overwhelmingly positive terms. It has also been noted that rituals which involve any kind of repetition such as chanting or rosary prayer help form resonance patterns in the brain which make this experience more likely to happen. So it would seem that the change many report after moments of deep prayer can also be connected to this kind of experience.

How can all of this be reconciled with the way in which the workings of the brain are generally conceived in the West? We have always had a simple idea of the machinery of the brain generating our consciousness. The image of our thoughts altering the very structure of our physical brains is one which raises many issues concerning mind-body interaction. Mind has usually been conceived as being entirely dependent upon matter. For us to consciously be able to exert influence through our thought patterns on the material brain would indicate that we have underestimated the place of consciousness. Indeed, many scientists today would say this is the case. For much of the last century our minds have been ignored by science because of its entirely subjective nature. Many scientists have almost written of consciousness as an evolutionary by-product or an illusion conjured by the brain. In recent times these views have been challenged and consciousness is being recognised as something more. The renowned physicist Roger Penrose has even put forward a quantum theory of mind that challenges most other classical scientific views. Some models have been formed of a possible two way process at work in the brain. Just as the brain can makes us think in a certain way our thoughts can make the brain work in a certain way. This appears to be more possible through sustained practise and effort. Consciousness could not be an illusion or useless by product if it can exert such an ability. This two way process can also help explain to us the workings of psychosomatic phenomenon. The influence the mind has over the brain may extend to wider aspects of the bodies general condition. It has long been recognised that moods and emotional temperament can exert influence over the health and life span of those holding them. The rarer and stranger forms of psychosomatic manifestations, such as stigmata, could also have light shone upon them by this kind of research.

All of these tests mainly show us two things. That change is possible in the way we think and perceive the world and that this change can be for the better. These are two facts that the Buddha must have believed in greatly to have first set out on his search. His path and meditative techniques have thus caused people living today to alter the way they think and see the world as much as in his own time.

Another interesting discovery included in all this research vindicates the Buddha even further. It has been discovered that the parts of the brain that deal with what is liked and what is wanted differ. Although we like most things we want to begin with, when we get used to wanting it we will eventually continue to want it whether we like it or not. This could go a long way in explaining some of humanities strangest behaviour. Considering this also makes the Buddha's choice of desire and want as the main cause of human suffering appear highly perceptive. Being trapped in a position of wanting something we don't like, never mind don't need, sounds bizarre as well as disturbing.

So the Buddha's method can make us happier and more capable of handling life. Gaining these abilities is still some distance away from the type of salvation from samsara that the goal of nirvana is promised to be. Becoming a little more cheerful in our world outlook or loosening our sense of self is still not sufficient enough to justify accepting his description of reality and our relation to it. The primacy of the mind is probably the most central factor in his teachings but the current understanding of the mind as the product of the physical brain differs from his conception of it as the unending chain of consciousness that continues after the death of the body. The relationship between damage to the physical brain and damage to the workings of the mind is taken as evidence in support of the current scientific view. Without a doubt this does display a deep connection between the brain and the mind, but if some kind of evidence were found that challenged the seemingly dependent nature of the mind upon the brain it would go a long way in backing up the Buddha's analysis of consciousness. It would also open up new possibilities on the conscious spectrum in regard to what nirvana is and what pursuing it can make us capable of.

It is true that evidence of this nature would be difficult to accept in the current Western climate. Many are sceptical even of the idea of consciousness not being generated by the brain, never mind continuing on into a different life. The belief in rebirth is often met with utter incredulousness or even contempt especially to these from a monotheistic heritage. In the West the attitude towards it seems to be one bordering upon hostility. This is most likely linked to our highly individualistic ethos and the way in which we value our individual identities. It is also probably because of the way in which it would deeply challenge many of our current world views. How could rebirth possibly fit in with our current understandings of evolutionary theory? Or variations in the number of living beings on the planet? Or what kind of mechanism could even enable this process?

The Sword From The Scabbard

Most monotheistic faiths consider this life the only one and so the one which God will use to judge our worthiness for Heaven. Perhaps the current hostility towards the belief in survival of consciousness into another life in this world can be traced back to this.

 The recent interest in hypno-regression can only add to this sense of disbelief and contempt. Watching celebrities talking about their past lives during hypnotic states is hardly within the realms of scientific analysis. The descriptions of these past lives are often amusing in their colourful detail and it is hard not to dismiss the sense of fantasy fulfilment that surrounds this kind of practise. There are normally always exotic locations and characters involved rather than ordinary people or occupations. Even if there was some truth in it, which there probably is not, we could hardly take it on board as any kind of reliable evidence. If a claim of this size is going to be made there had better at least be some indication of substantiation.

 At a certain level it is perfectly possible to apply the teachings of the Buddha to daily life without needing any reference at all to previous existences or new ones to come. We have seen the effect it can have upon the practitioners thought patterns within this life, whether the individual believes in the possibility of rebirth or not. In fact some recognised Buddhist authorities have even discouraged belief in rebirth entirely. Stephen Batchelor has advised practitioners not to believe in it because of all the speculation and mystery that would follow in the wake of its discovery. Rebirth, he believes, is probably a part of the Buddha's cultural baggage and most likely untrue. Another off putting element of this kind of belief is those desiring knowledge about their previous lives or their next life. Such speculation and fantasising is entirely inimical to the focus on the current moment and respect for reality that lies at the core of the Buddha's teaching. Perhaps it is best to approach his dharma without any belief in older lives or ones to come because of the increased effort the practitioner will give it, understanding this life to be the only chance to put his teachings into practise. Others understand rebirth as a metaphor for all of the changes we endure during this one life. Although we share a line of continuation the person we are now is not the one we were ten years ago or are going to be ten years time. As true as this is it still seems a feeble version of what is commonly understood as rebirth in Buddhist philosophy. Batchelors belief that rebirth was only a part of the Buddha's cultural baggage also seems hard to reconcile with some of the other elements of his life. The Buddha never had any trouble disregarding other received elements of his culture, such as the eternal Self and the caste system. What he could not find reasonable evidence in support of he would not teach. Why retain the belief in rebirth and the continuation of consciousness? It does not sit well with his teachings, taken as a whole, if he taught his followers something he had entirely taken on faith. It could even bring into question other elements of his teachings. If he were mistaken on this point then perhaps his description of reality or explanation of nirvana were mistaken. Most people assume that since there is no evidence either way or that this element of the Buddha-Dharma that is taken entirely on faith. It can be explained within the realms of Buddhist philosophy but is still a huge leap from current scientific understandings of consciousness. This in turn raises the un-Buddha like attitude of ignoring what has emerged as the result of rational and scientifically sound research. It would remain this way expect for bringing into account the life work of a man called Ian Stevenson and the conclusions his dedicated research has pointed to. After careful analysis of his discoveries it tips the scale of opinion more clearly in one direction and it is only how his research can be reconciled with the predominant world view held in the West today that needs to be adequately addressed.

 Stevenson was born in Montreal, Canada and it was here in 1943 that he received his M.D. from McGill University, graduating at the top of his class. In 1960 Dr. Stevenson published a paper concerning his study on the topic of reincarnation. This attracted the interest of a man called Chester Carlson who decided, after studying the paper, to fund more of Stevenson's research in India and Sri Lanka. His work involved the study of young children who claimed to remember memories of previous lives without the need for any kind of hypnosis or regression. The children he would investigate would usually talk of the memories between the ages of two and four and normally stop by the age of seven or eight. The cases he was most interested in were the ones in which the children could give enough detail for the claimed previous personality to be identified and their homes and families found.

Carlson was the millionaire who changed technology and copyright law by forming the Xerox Corporation. The invention of the copying machine earned him about one hundred and fifty million dollars, of which he donated around one hundred million of to charitable causes, especially those supporting the civil rights movement in America. In 1963 Carlson died and Stevenson was shocked to discover that he had left him one million dollars to endow a Chair at the University of Virginia and another million to help him continue his research.

Stevenson's work is highly meticulous and packed with details concerning each case. He was always careful to describe his research as cases suggestive of reincarnation, well aware of how people would react to the conclusions he was pointing to. His work has been only published for the scientific community and so does not make easy reading. By his work being limited to this form of publishing brings two main benefits. It is the scientific community that is the ultimate test of his research. Should they study the evidence and be able to dismiss it or explain it as something other than what appears then it is healthy science. Releasing his work to the general public without such scrutiny or sharing amongst his peers is taking a huge risk. Should it gain publicity then his name will be tied to this research and then brought into question if a fellow scientist is able to explain away the evidence. The other benefit of keeping it amongst scientific circles is to avoid the sensationalism such research can create and the adverse effects this can lead to. By not publicising his research loudly it also prevents any accusations of him searching for fame. Although the result of this policy has meant he has not gotten as much recognition as he could have it also means that it is possible to take his work much more seriously.

Although his research has taken place predominantly in societies that already believe in rebirth such as Asia and among Alaskan tribes he believes the phenomenon can be uncovered anywhere we really look for it. The reason it is easier to find in these places is that people are more willing to listen to their children's claims of a previous life. Or at least not dismiss them as completely imaginative. Often the children are able to name where it is they previously came from and their previous family members. They pester their parents to take them back to their homes and often out of curiosity or to quieten the child they will. When they reach these places the child is normally able to remember their home and even identify family members.

As an example that includes many of the basics of each of these cases are the events that surrounded a young girl called Sukla who was born in Kampa, a village in India. She was the daughter of Sri K.N. Sen Gupta. When Sukla was only about one and a half years old she was observed cradling a block of wood and addressing it by the name of Minu. When asked who Minu was she replied that it was her daughter. Over the next few years she gradually revealed more information about who Minu was and began to speak of memories of a previous life. She spoke of having a husband and named his younger brothers as Khetu and Karuna. All of these people lived, as she claimed to once have, in a place called Rathtala, Bhatpara. This village was only eleven miles from Kampa and the Gupta family Sukla was born into knew of it but although they had heard of Bhatpara, they were unfamiliar with a district within it called Rathtala or of people with the names given by Sukla. Despite this she still developed an overwhelming desire to visit Bhatpara and claimed she could lead the way to he father-in-law's home. In time she began to insist that she would go alone if her family would not take her.

Her father became concerned about all of this and spoke to several of his friends about it, including one Sri S.C. Pal who he worked with at the railways. Pal lived near Bhatpara and had relatives who lived in the village. Through them he found out that there was indeed a section called Rathtala and in it lived a man of the name Khetu. Pal also found out that Khetu once had a sister-in-law called Mana, who had died a number of years ago. She had left behind an infant girl called Minu. When this information reached Sukla's father he became more interested in visiting Bhatpara and confirming all of this for himself. He arranged a visit to this household through its head, Sri Amritalal Chakravarty, and a number of his family, including Sukla, went to visit.

At the house Sukla showed some confusion as to where the entrance was. It was later confirmed that the entrance to the house had been changed since the death of Mana from the front to the side of the building. While inside the house Minu arrived and Sukla became emotional at the sight of her. Although the room was crowded when Sukla was asked to identify who she claimed was once her husband she pointed to Haridhan Chakravarty, the father of Minu and former husband of Mana. She also pointed to Khetu and identified him as the uncle of Minu. The other brother entered the house and after a few minutes asked who Sukla thought he was. She answered correctly that he was Karuna, her younger brother-in-law. It was more remarkable considering that Karuna had always been known by the nickname Kuti. Not even his neighbours had been aware that his real name was Karuna. He and Mana had been close before her death and she was one of the few people who were aware of what his real name was. Sukla also went on to recognise Mana's mother-in-law and one of her aunts. It was with this aunt Mana had left the house with on the day she died and who she had made promise to take care of Minu as she was dying.

After this some members of Mana's family came to visit Sukla in her hometown. Before Mana's husband arrived on one occasion she made the family prepare him prawns and buli, which she claimed was his favorite food. Upon arrival he confirmed this. When Sukla was asked if Minu was her only child she told of having a previous child who had died in infancy. This was confirmed by the relatives of Mana. Other details she could remember was certain items of clothing that once belonged to Mara and that she and her husband had onced lived in Kharagpur for a time. She remembered details about animals that the family had once owned including the colour of two of their cows.

This was one of Stevenson's earliest cases and while investigating it he has met all of those involved. As in some of the more interesting cases he has tried his best to keep in touch with those involved, both out of personal and scientific interest. Sukla continued to receive visits from her claimed former family members for many years. She showed great attachment to Mana's former husband and daughter and appeared to be emotionally attached to them. It was not until she grew older that she began to let go, as is common in most cases, of her former life and accept her new identity. Visits from the former family lessened for a number of reasons, including her old husband's new wife disliking him visiting her and her own personal feelings of inadequacy arising from the case.

This is a good example of the basics of what Stevenson seeks before recording a case. A young child claims memories of a previous life which can be later confirmed by those he or she knows. Stevenson interviews all of those involved he can and then considers any alternate possibilities to explain the occurrences. In this case the close proximity of the villages could mean that there was some other way of Sukla discovering this information. On the other hand it could not explain the extent of Sukla's knowledge or why she would want to trick everyone into believing what she said. Remember that Sukla was five when she first visited Bhatpara. Some might claim the entire incident was in some way staged or faked. The problem with this explanation again is that of motivation. Often these cases are deeply difficult for those involved as the child is torn between two families. The search for fame cannot be easily used as a motivation either since rebirth is common belief in such parts of the world as India. It is also considered bad luck to remember a previous life in India which is why some families there do not like to hear their children talk of such things. In some cases Stevenson or some members of his research team have actually managed to get to a subject before either of the families involved has met. In these cases they can watch such early interactions themselves and gather valuable evidence. The dedication and effort that goes into his work is obvious from the level of detail collected in each case. So far he and his team have managed to gather details of almost three thousand cases, most with as much, if not more, detail than the one given above.

Tom Shroder is an American journalist who decided to accompany Stevenson on one of his research trips and probe him about his discoveries. This resulted in his book *Old Souls*. He came with him to visit families in Beirut and India and upon returning to America visited a case by himself, accompanying a child in Virginia who remembered owning a farm located near to where he lived. Stevenson referred this case to Shroder to give him a chance to visit such an occurrence alone. In the end Shroder comes across as convinced of Stevenson's research although he can offer no explanation of how such occurrences are taking place, but does point to some of the gaps and mysteries inherent within modern science as a starting point.

One of the issues Stevenson raises with Shroder is the non-acceptance of all his work by the mainstream community. No scientists attack his meticulous methods and dedication to scientific principles but only the conclusions of his research. Few, if any, can offer any kind of alternate explanation to what is happening to these children within the limits of modern scientific understanding. Those who are highly sceptical of any conclusions involving rebirth can only come up with an explanation involving some kind of extra-sensory perception. This is a long distance away from a normal explanation. As well as this, the high level of identification with the memories the child displays would seem to indicate otherwise. Some mainstream scientists, however, recognise that Stevenson has discovered something of note. Carl Sagan, the renowned astrophysicist and committed debunker of all things paranormal, has even cited Stevenson's kind of research as worthy of further study.

Another interesting aspect of Stevenson's work concerns the placement of birthmarks upon the children and their apparent positional relevance to wounds inflicted upon the previous personality. An unusually high number of the cases involved report some form of violent or sudden death. It has been speculated that perhaps that the reason why these children can remember elements of their previous life is due to the premature and sudden break with it. An example of this is that of the birthmark on the chest of Hanumant Saxena and how it corresponds to the wounds left by a shotgun blast on the same location by the person, Maha Ram Singh, Hanumant claimed to have once been. It should be noted that to this date, although there are some ideas and known influences, there is still no consensus on what it is that causes specific birthmarks to appear on certain locations. The main importance of this kind of evidence is that it is a step further in support of rebirth as a valid explanation for these occurrences. Here are more than just the memories of a child that fade in time, but a physical manifestation in support of such memory. Some could try and criticise it and say that perhaps the child weaves a story around their birthmark but this theory falls apart in the face of the kind of verification that can be conducted on the details given by the child.

Stevenson was cautious in his conclusions, aware of how much they challenge the accepted scientific orthodoxy. He states in Tom Shroder's book that given the wealth of evidence collected it would be perfectly reasonable for someone now to believe in rebirth. He considers previous personalities as a third shaping factor, along with genetics and the environment, in human development. He also believed that perhaps it should be also taken into account in the fields of birth defects, abnormalities and numerous other unsolved problems in the fields of psychology and medicine. He concludes in one of the general discussions in his collected work that it is possible that humanity is undergoing a dual evolution-one involving our bodies and one of our minds. This is probably the closest to a wild statement to be found in all of his work. The tragedy of all his efforts is that while one half of the world dismisses it without looking at it, the other half already believes in rebirth so is without any need of convincing.

Stevenson died on February 8th 2007 in Virginia. His life work is continued by several members of his research team. Where he recognised the biggest hole in his discoveries was in the lack of any adequate explanation for how the mind could possibly travel from the deceased body into a new one. Perhaps that is where the Buddha's explanation of a continuing line of energy shaped by habitual patterns could come in.

One possible explanation for the lack of acceptance for Stevenson's research and hostility towards the idea of rebirth in the West has more to do with the Christian world view that forms the roots of modern science than scientific discovery itself. The classical scientific understanding of reality has its basis in the Newtonian universe. In turn this vision of the universe, as we saw earlier, derives from Christian conceptions of reality. In this view God created the world and placed us into it. Current understandings of science involve us, using the tools of perception and analysis, watching and trying to understand how this world works. Science still retains this Christian view of us placed in the world, but able to separate ourselves from it in order to determine its workings. Rebirth would challenge this image of our minds as separate from the processes of the world. If the mind that is being reborn can alter the shape or feature of the person being born then it questions this objective and separate nature of the mind. If it can influence the world around us in such a way then it is not as trapped in us as the image of the soul would have. Many scientists still hold onto a concept of the universe that is, although atheist, Christian orientated, so in this sense rebirth is contrary to the scientific world view but not to the discoveries of science itself. In fact, certain other discoveries of science also happen to be breaking down this barrier between our minds and the world around us.

Einstein's discovery of relativity drastically altered the way in which we understand the world. It can in fact be understood as the body of concepts that blew the Newtonian worldview out of the water. No longer was the universe a great clockwork with steady rules and constant conditions. Instead we have new stranger understandings of gravity, time and light and their relationship to each other. Many scientists today show concern at the fact that although discoveries such as relativity are not new, very few people in the general public seem to be aware of their implications. The fact that time runs faster at the base of Mount Everest than at the tip or that gravity alters the shape of time and space often seems to shock people with its strangeness. Our Christian-derived steady, logical view of the world-out-there seems to be increasingly becoming shaky as scientific research probes further into it.

Even the corner stone of scientific research, objectivity, has been deeply undermined by some of the most important areas of discovery. In the 18th and 19th centuries it once seemed as if science would be able to cure all of the world's problems and explain all of its mysteries. The steady view of the universe that dominated meant that it was only a matter of time before research would be able to determine all of the rules that governed its internal interactions. By the end of the 19th century it was thought that the discipline of physics had sorted out all of the main workings of the universe and that all was left to discover was small details. Not only did relativity undermine this view but so did what has become known as the quantum revolution, and its concept of the implicated observer.

The Sword From The Scabbard

Between 1911 and 1913 experiments had shown that electrons seemed to be able to slide between orbits around the nucleus of an atom. The atom was what scientists had previously identified as the building blocks that came together to form all matter. At its centre sat the nucleus, which was formed of neutrons and protons, and around this flew electrons in an orbit. The strange thing about the behaviour of these electrons in was that they seemed to be hopping from one orbit to another instantaneously. There was no movement from one orbit to another but rather a sudden hop. By the 1930's more contradiction seemed to appear with electron movement irreconcilable with their momentum and ending up where it was impossible for them to be. This eventually culminated in what is known as the uncertainty principle. Apparently it is not possible to state both the momentum and the position of these particles, not because of a lack in sophisticated enough tools, but because this is not how this world operates. This is only the tip of the iceberg in quantum weirdness. It should also be noted that discoveries of this kind are some of the ones that corroded the confidence that was held in science throughout the 20th century. Uncertainty such as this seemed to diminish sciences claim on hard facts and irrefutable truths. That, as well as the levels of destruction and pain that were visited upon human life as a result of certain scientific discoveries.

The area of quantum physics that has caused the most amount of controversy and heated debate is, undoubtedly, what is known as the two-slit experiment. Basically it involves the behaviour, once again, of tiny particles such as electrons. In this case they are fired by a specially designed gun toward an image screen that will pick up where it has landed. Between the gun and the image screen is a board with two slits in it. When the particles are fired individually at the screen it was expected that they should, by travelling through both slits, form two lines on the image screen. Instead, doubtless to the shock of all involved, they formed what is known as an interference pattern. This is more like the image that would be picked up if a wave of something was thrown at the screen. For example, if water were to flow towards the two slits it would go through both and come out the other side interfering with itself and thereby creating a spread out interference pattern on the screen. Individual particles being shot at the screen, like marbles, should not be able to create an interference pattern but should be forming two lines, in the same vague shape as the slits on the board. Scientists decided it would be a good idea to watch the particle travel through the slit and see what kind of shape it takes in order to create such a pattern. When a measuring device was set up to watch the particle travel at this point something entirely unexpected occurred. The particles retained their shape and travelled through the slits as was originally expected. When the measuring device was turned of or removed the particles made the interference pattern but when the particle was watched it made the expected two slit pattern. What is going on here is yet to receive any explanatory consensus. The mystery lies in how or why the particle adopts some kind of wave form when reaching the slits and image screen. Or, more importantly, why and how it changes behaviour when it is being measured or observed? What has the act of us observing the particle got anything to do with its choice of behaviour? How does it know when to behave like a particle and when to behave like a wave and why does it care?

This is what is meant by the implicated observer. By merely observing the experiment we are altering its outcome, therefore undermining the objectivity science prides itself on. In this case there is no way to become entirely objective since watching the experiment means participating in it. So not only do the results of this experiment challenge conventional understandings of the world around us but they also challenge the nature of the scientific method itself.

This experiment was first conducted decades ago and the various explanations put forward for it since then have been stranger than some science fiction. Most interpretations of it have the particle entering some state of potentiality when it is in its wave form. Some maintain that when it is measured or observed it collapses from this state of potential positions into only one. This is the one we see when we watch the particle travel through the slits. Others think that the other potential positions in the wave form universes of their own that run parallel to our own in a great multi-verse. These are actually some of the more conservative theories. What it is that causes the wave to collapse into a single particle has been variously described as measurement, observation and even in some cases consciousness.

 Since our entire universe is formed by this micro world it all brings into question some of our deepest held convictions about the nature of reality. It has always been recognised that the way we see the world differs from how it really exists in itself but to say that it actually changes form or comes into existence because of us observing it is very different. Would this mean that when we are not looking at something it ceases to exist?

 Whatever these discoveries turn out to mean they are now impossible to reconcile with the mechanistic and deterministic universe that frightened so many with its cold barrenness. Instead we could have something even weirder on our hands and much more mysterious. In a way discoveries such as this, although more accepted than the idea of rebirth, are as strange as it. The image of our minds playing a role in the creation of the universe around us, like rebirth, is also a common theme in Eastern philosophical traditions, not one of the least being the Buddha-Dharma.

 An interesting variation of the two-slit experiment is the delayed choice version. This was first suggested by theoretical physicist, John Wheeler, and then carried out in a terrestrial laboratory by Carroll Alley and his colleagues at the University of Maryland. Wheeler suggested replacing the image screen with a kind of blind that can be opened and closed at will. The idea is to open the blind after the particle has passed the slit board and see what form it takes. Wheeler believed that when the blind was opened it would turn from a wave into a particle, as indeed it turned out to be. This means that it travelled through the slits as a wave but then collapsed into a particle afterwards. The main point of interest concerning this version of the experiment is that the newly collapsed particle must now choose one of the slits on the board for itself to have travelled through. As we know, however, it travelled through both as a wave. Yet, when the experiment was conducted the particles that were picked up clearly had chosen one slit over another for themselves to come through. Now, what exactly does this mean?

 What it does not mean, according to the scientist and writer Paul Davies, is any form of simplistic backward causation but rather something much more elusive. The particle does not exist as wave or particle on its own since these states only come to into existence through the experiment. What the experiment does seem to suggest is that the actions and participation of the observer not only affects the shape of reality in the present but in the past. Continuing with this line of thought does not only mean that we can affect the shape of the recent past, as in the delayed choice two-slit experiment but further back into the remote past. Wheeler has even hypothesised an experiment at an astronomical scale involving photons headed towards earth that would prove participatory influence on events billions of years in the past.

Wheeler, and many other modern scientists, have suggested a new vision of the cosmos involving its observers as being participators in the very shaping of it. This is radical in that it forms a vision of the universe involving life and the mind as indispensable to its formation both now and in the past before our existence. Humanity is no longer a by product of a cold and dead cosmos but an integral element in its creation and formation.

This can be tied into what is known as the anthropic principle. This principle points out that if any scientific law or rule in the universe had been slightly different then it would have been impossible for life to form. The odds of there being a universe perfect for the manifestation of life are astronomically slim. Some take this for evidence of a divine creator while others tie it into the multi-verse theory. Wheelers experiment could explain it within a closed system that does not require any outside influence or explanation at all. According to this outlook the conventional linear understanding of the formation of the world and us (cosmos-life-mind) actually becomes a loop (cosmos-life-mind-cosmos). The universe creates us and then we in turn create it. In this understanding a universe cannot come into existence without a mind of some kind to form it. The anthropic principle is explained because our minds will only form a universe that can evolve with the ability to create them. Unlike the void formed by classical science this new understanding of reality is teeming with and dependent upon life. Wheeler rejected the concept of a universe as a machine driven by laws but posits a participatory universe that is self synthesising.

Thomas Kuhn wrote of paradigm shifts, in which new evidence coming to light shifts the world view from one phase into the next. Relativity and the quantum revolution is the evidence that motivated one of these shifts, although it has yet to reach the level of common knowledge. Another term connected to these kinds of changes is cognitive dissonance. What this refers to is the inability of those who are attached to the old way of viewing the universe to accept the extent of the change new evidence reveals. Atheists would claim modern day Christians could be described in such terms, but today the newest discoveries of science and comparative religious studies would indicate it is they who suffer from it, with their faith in the now defunct classical scientific worldview. New discoveries and beliefs are not suddenly accepted because it is obvious to everyone involved that they are true, but unfortunately only through time, when those who hold to the older views no longer form the establishment. The same can be said for most areas of knowledge and research.

The type of theories and experiments that are now being discussed in the most respected of scientific establishments paint a picture of the universe both mystifying and tantalising. Much of what we consider normal is under attack and what was once considered outside the realms of possibility is now seeping in. Perhaps one day there will even be room for the kind of research Ian Stevenson spent his life compiling.

As for the Buddha things seem to be travelling almost eerily in his direction. The two elements of his explanation of human consciousness and its relationship to the world that could be considered more on the supernatural side seem to be finding some real evidence. His description of the mind as being what helps form the external world might be something similar to Wheeler's theories on how observers influence the formation of the world around them. Even the very basics of the two-slit experiment indicate a tighter connection between our minds and the external world that was previously thought. Even Ricard, the scientist turned monk, has mentioned the similarities between the interpretation of quantum physics known as the Copenhagen Interpretation and Buddhist philosophy. As for rebirth Stevenson's work provides ample material in support. His identification of birthmarks and certain characteristics in the involved personalities concurs with the Buddha's explanation of how past lives influence the current one through the formation of habitual patterns.

Again it should be noted that conventional modern science still grapples with the nature of consciousness and the relationship of the mind with the body. There simply are no theories on how our subjective experience of reality comes about or definitions on exactly what it is. Within the paradigm of conventional modern science it almost does not even have a place.

At the end of the previous chapter I stated that there should be at the very least no evidence directly contradicting the Buddha's teachings. Even, perhaps, that given his empirical mindset and respect for truth it might be possible to find evidence in support of his analysis of reality. Given that all that is written in this chapter is only a small glimpse into the fields they represent I think it possible to look at modern scientific discovery and from a Buddhist point of view be satisfied. As stated earlier this is no basis for belief in itself but is deeply encouraging, not to mention highly interesting.

The Sword From The Scabbard

6

FOR THE WORLD TODAY

Most people are unaware of most of the newest discoveries about the effects long term meditation or dharma practise can have upon the mind yet interest in Buddhism seems to be growing throughout the West. Only a few decades ago knowledge of it was highly limited but today dharma or meditation centres are now available in most major cities. Numerous celebrities have taken up the practise in a devoted and genuine way. Richard Gere credits it with saving him from becoming what he was once described as an asshole Others with a similar interest have included Orlando Bloom and, in his own amusing way, Stephen Seagal. In France some estimate that Buddhists are soon set to outnumber Protestants and Jews, becoming France's third largest religious following.

In part this may be due to the good publicity Buddhism and its representatives seem to gain for themselves. They appear to lack the hypocrisy that has turned so many off the Western religions. Indeed, history does seem to back up this view, there being no Buddhist version of the crusades or the witch hunts.

A great example of this good publicity can be seen in the world's fascination with the Fourteenth Dalai Lama, the leader-in-exile of Tibetan Buddhism. Even the annexation of his homeland by China has not shaken his Buddhist faith in non-violence and compassion. In today's world, where so many leaders are so ready to invade other nations for what they perceive as the common good it is no wonder that he attracts such fascination. While others are so ready to wage violence upon others in the name of noble causes he occupies a radical position in his belief in the futility of war. While some deride his position as hopelessly naïve or ineffectual he believes otherwise. Violence cannot be used as a tool of policy simply because it never works. This is a lesson many in greater positions of power have yet to learn. In today's world politicians often attempt to unite their supporters through the hatred of some perceived enemy. Someone must be chosen to play this role of Satan or evil-doer in order to affirm the belief of themselves as representatives of the good. It is noticeable that traditions without monotheistic backgrounds are not so quick to use such rhetoric. The Buddhist tradition of the Dalai Lama has no such evil figure, which is a policy reflected in his understandings of the world. His homeland and people may be suffering but the purity and beauty of their culture is preserved in this stance. Due to the size of the market China is now opening to foreign investment, other powers are reluctant to condemn their treatment of the Tibetans. History, however, shows that such attempts at cultural eradication and the subjection of other populations often has a way of backfiring. In years to come China could come to regret its heavy handed policies. The Dalai Lama's tireless promotion of peaceful and benevolent causes around the world also makes him difficult to criticise. Indeed, most Chinese propaganda portraying him as a separatist and terrorist feels surreal in its own naivety.

After a recent visit to a Belfast church by the Dalai Lama, a minister voiced concern at the size of the crowd who had come to see him compared to that which visited the church each week. Of course his celebrity status has to be taken into account, but it still difficult to see many other religious leaders attracting such publicity. In a place where religion was so abused over the years as Belfast, perhaps it is not difficult to understand such curiosity about someone who has stuck by their religious principles.

This growing interest in the Buddha-Dharma can be seen as a symptom of the nihilism that has gripped the West. The withdrawing of conventional motivations has encouraged people to look or at least be curious about other ways and understandings of life. Many have already ended their search with the Buddha while others choose something different. Of course there are those who lament this growth of interest in traditions outside of the West. In many cases this can sound like the old school chauvinism that has been such a terrible part of Western culture. People cringe at the thought of others searching out answers from locations they deem unworthy or unorthodox. The only valid answers, they feel, can only to be found within their own traditions.

As clarified earlier, the Buddha's path is one open for people at all times, but it is likely that there are some times for which it is more appropriate or easier to understand. Today's world is probably the best example of one of these times. He particularly targeted the human problems that seem to be the cause of much of the suffering in the modern world. Our sense of nihilism, meaningless, existential boredom and confusion about what should be believed are tackled directly by the path he laid out for humanity to follow. He promised an end to our confusion and suffering and, as the evidence appears to confirm, he discovered it.

Where this could be highly beneficial to ourselves and society is in tackling the health related problems of the depression that is expected to reach record levels in years to come. Uni-polar depression's most noted aspect, other than the drop in quality of daily life, is its effect upon heart disease. If the growing sales of anti-depressants are anything to go by then some alternate solutions are well needed. It must be wondered if today there are executives at the top of pharmaceutical companies who are looking forward to the rise in sales just around the corner. The benefit of the happiness that can be gained through meditative techniques is that it is more permanent and less reliant upon a prescription. If any government is searching for a solution that does not involve the mass distribution of anti-depressants then perhaps it is here they should look.

It was once noticed that some of those who were currently practising the Buddha-Dharma had at some point in the past experimented with mind altering chemicals. Although some self proclaimed guru's jumped upon this as evidence that drug induced experiences were actually examples of what enlightenment or nirvana felt like, it would seem what these people had really learnt was how different the mind could become at times. They also may have realised that true happiness can be suddenly gained by the mind without any external change, only a kind of inner change. It is probably this that influenced their decision to become Buddhists rather than any tastes of nirvana. Their experiences have made them more acutely aware of the subjective aspect of reality. The widespread use of recreational drugs today, however, is a matter of concern. Although many attitudes opposed to drugs are exaggerated or unrealistic, the acceptance of drug use as normal is bad. Most casual drug users are well aware of the damaging aspects of this behaviour but persist anyway. People losing their days and memory to marijuana use or their temperament to ecstasy consider it justified considering the gains they feel they make. Namely some entertainment and escape from boredom. The temporary release from ordinary life that is granted from use appears to be more attractive to most people than anything else. Conventional religion does not posit what many recreational drug users would consider as any kind of realistic alternative or solution. Usually when help is considered needed it is only in the most extreme of cases. Perhaps it is the void between using out of boredom and extreme cases that the Buddha's advice can be applied.

In a way there are similarities between drug use and the application of the Buddha-Dharma. Both seek to alter the way in which the user thinks by changing the way in which their minds work. Many religious ceremonies and practises are known to involve the use of mind altering chemicals in order to bring about a particular experience. But while drug use is over quickly and temperamental by nature, the changes the Buddha's teachings make are permanent and steady. Those who use drugs habitually do so because they enjoy the way in which their minds operate during the experience. Most are unaware that methods exist which can alter the mind without the use of extraneous substances. Many even seek an experience through drugs to widen their minds or learn something, as is supposed to occur through the use of hallucinogenic drugs such as LSD or magic mushrooms. This kind of philosophy once played a huge role in the counter cultural movement of the 1960's. Most adherents were very aware of the connection between drug use and spirituality. Timothy Leary, the father figure of the 1960's counter cultural movement, equated the experiences induced by LSD with the concepts of enlightenment and nirvana found in Eastern philosophy. There may be some truth in this given the almost identical descriptions given of spiritual and LSD induced experiences. Where criticism could be laid against the use of LSD as a shortcut to spiritual experience is in that it does not take into account other important factors of spirituality, such as dedication, faith and ethical behaviour.

The Buddha would have had no time for these methods of trying to deal with life. The dependence upon chemicals to regulate moods or manufacture spiritual experiences creates a crutch that can be difficult to live without. In time the user will only associate feeling good with the particular chemical and become annoyed if it is removed from them. Those who expect some kind of life changing experience through drugs are looking in the wrong direction. What is experienced through them can only ever be temporary and so loses its resonance in time. The Buddha's method may take longer and more effort but he would have said it was worth it. The levels of happiness his path opens one up to only deepen and broaden with time. Another detrimental effect of the habitual use of drugs is the damage the brain can endure. The more dangerous effects of ecstasy have already been mentioned. If long term use does have the ability to cancel the brains ability to be happy then any chance of attaining a lasting inner happiness is reduced by each pill. The way in which weed seems to suck away time and motivation makes it a killer for the effort that is such an important part of the Buddha's path. Or life for that matter.

The psychological root of the regular use of drugs can probably be found in the same place that motivated many in the past to follow the Buddha's path. It does seem to indicate a yearning from the user to change the way in which they think from how it works mundanely to something different. Perhaps the use of drugs sometimes does gives glimpses to a hidden, fuller reality. This would find backing when it is considered how the use of drugs is often seen as a temporary escape from the self. If the self is an illusion then it means temporarily perceiving reality without that illusion. Unfortunately for the user, the chemical normally gives rise to illusions of its own.

It is interesting to wonder what the Buddha would have made of the various ideologies that grew to dominate the 20th century. Would these have been examples of what he meant by wrong views? Indeed, there very nature does seem to run counter to the core of his teachings. Rather than transcending the conceptual mind they lock the world into a network of concepts and ideas. When an individual was caught within this network of beliefs it often seemed difficult for them to escape it.

One renowned Buddhist teacher has said that the idea of happiness is a very dangerous thing. The happiness the Buddha taught is available only in the here and now but to believe that your happiness lies in the future at some point, after you have rearranged your surroundings or fulfilled some set of goals often leads to disaster. The attraction of happiness is so deep that often people will stop at no means to reach their goal. The nature of our thoughts and projections of the future are deeply flawed, which normally means that when we get where we wanted to go it is always different than expected.

Communism is probably the easiest example of this delusional search for happiness. The belief and faith held by millions in some future perfected communist state justified the destruction of millions of lives in the pursuit of contentment and fairness. The same can be said for the Nazi project. Or even for the neoconservatives who believed the invasion of Iraq would usher in a golden age of liberal democracy. Again and again history had torn down all such utopian projects and rejected such grand attempts at mass happiness. Politics requires pragmatism and compromise rather than blinkered ideology. Enveloping the world in a blanket of pre-established concepts and opinions without opening to reality has proven to be disastrous wherever it has been practised. It has been seen earlier how all of these ideologies were little more than corruptions of Christianity and manifestations of the repressed religious drive. They were religions without any kind of transcendent element and so doomed. It is likely the Buddha would have dismissed the very nature of ideology itself as hopelessly dangerous. Certainly many Buddhist leaders today do.

The Sword From The Scabbard

The weak form of happiness so many seem to be chasing after in the form of fulfilled wants appears immature compared to the Buddha's version of how true satisfaction is reached. Realising this could in turn this could help counter the consumerist urge that is so much a part of modern life. What is known as affluenza, the disappointing and short term nature of the pleasure connected to purchasing goods, could be combated by the adoption of the Buddha's advice and worldview. Searching for contentment or happiness in such places appears to be exactly what the Buddha described as delusional practises.

A reduction in the levels of consumerism could have untold benefits in the world around us. The current ecological crisis has been created by the unsustainable levels of consumption humanity has reached. Some argue against anything that counters these levels of consumption as bad for business or the economy. It feels like a false argument when the fact that their won't be any business or type of economy left if we continue on this path is brought into consideration. The Buddha's focus on the delusional nature of desire and craving make it best suited to offer insights into how we can control ourselves and our more destructive urges. Perhaps those businesses and individuals who continue to destroy the world in the name of profit are perfect examples of delusional thinking. Surely profit should be possible without the destruction of life. Or to be more accurate profit is surely impossible with the destruction of life.

What the Buddha's teachings also do is enter philosophy back into the lives of ordinary people. In the past Western philosophy was designed to offer consolation and advice to those who heard it but today it is so far removed from daily life as to be inapplicable. Buddhist philosophy, rather than abstract speculation, developed over time to defend it from attack form other schools and so has become rich and deep, as well as interesting. All of it is designed to assist in the individuals practise and daily life rather than as musings on the nature of the universe. Those who develop an interest in Buddhism often start out of admiration of its philosophical discourse and beautiful use of metaphor.

The modern fascination with the trivial that seems to be such a part of consumerist culture has lead to what has been described as an obsession with distraction. This isn't difficult to spot in the amount of hours devoted to DVD's, video games, iPod's, television shows or other forms of entertainment. Although there is nothing wrong in enjoying these activities, a life filled with nothing else feels worthless and trivial in itself. At least practise of the Buddha-Dharma injects an activity into life that go's beyond such limited pursuits.

 The excesses of the cult of the self that has grown to dominance from the beginning of the 20th century are prime targets for change under Buddhist practise. Since the self is considered an illusion then a lot of the self searching that seems to motivate so many lives appears a flawed exercise. It is letting go of the search for and promotion of the self that true knowledge and contentment lies. It has already been described how our highly developed sense of individuality and personality is the result of our Christian heritage. The Buddha's message is addressed to us individually, but actually describes our make up as utterly unlike this image of the autonomous individual. In this sense it is the antidote to the problems that come with the overdeveloped impression of self. The sense of alienation that has been such a part of the modern world experience has been caused by the focus upon ourselves that developed in the withdrawal of higher causes. This alienation can be countered in the explanation of reality's interdependent nature given by the Buddha. Truly realising that we are not autonomous individuals but pieces of the environment around us helps us feel more at home in the world we are presented with. Enlightenment rests in understanding that we are not nor ever will be the one. We are not even a one. It also goes a long way in explaining human behaviour if we drop the pretence that any of us are purely logical and rational individuals. Such a being would require complete objectivity. Logic and rationality have their fields, but they are not the forces that guide life.

 Some may feel that the doctrine of no-self is a threat to liberal culture in its seemingly dismissive nature of the individual. For several reasons this is inaccurate. For one thing, the individual is essential for dharma practise, since it is people who must work on themselves. Another point that must be considered is that individuality is not as real in modern culture as is sometimes claimed. In many cases it can be compared to the *Life of*

Brian '….we are all individuals' sketch. We are much more like herd animals than is often admitted. It has also been noticed that the deeper developed individualism of the West has a higher level of neurosis and insecurities as its result. This is another symptom of the cult of the individual.

 Both of these points help shed light on how applicable the Buddha-Dharma is to today's atomised world and the reason for the surge in its popularity. The changes in the world when the Buddha lived also helped heighten this image of the individual alone. Our generation and his are similar then, in that the older spiritual solutions were geared towards structured communities rather than individuals, becoming because of it less applicable to daily life. It is ironic then that it is the promotion of the self in society that prepares it perfectly for the Buddha's message and its inherent abnegation of the self. That individuality is not as real as advertised is something anyone in the medical or social field can testify to. We all really do seem under inspection to be enticed by similar factors and motivated by common desires. Perhaps, like the Buddha's early followers, learning that the self is not as real or permanent as thought will feel like the lifting of a burden. In modern culture where so much pressure and stress is tied to life, this will be even more so. The West prides itself on pushing boundaries but perhaps there are elements of the Buddha-Dharma, such as this, that are almost too radical for it.

 The successful nature of cognitive therapy in dealing with psychological issues and conditions even has its precedent in Buddhist practise. Although it remains controversial in psychiatric circles its success rate has meant it cannot be dismissed. Its simple advice, such as countering bad thoughts with good ones, works on a similar understanding of habitual patterns of thinking as in Buddhism. Others criticise this as too simplistic an interpretation of thought processes and believe it to lead to superficial cures. They seek out repressed memories and debilitating complexes to explain such problems. Strange and shocking secrets are supposed to lure in the deepest recesses of the self, manifesting as these inner conflicts. What about the Oedipus complex, penis envy or the other leftovers from Freudian sexual obsession? Surely these need to be confronted and dealt with in order for the patient to get on with life. The evidence would appear otherwise.

The Sword From The Scabbard

The solutions advocated by cognitive therapy may appear simplistic but they are successful. Perhaps we are not as deep and dark as was once thought. Buddhists concur with Freud in that there are regions of the mind we are not aware of but they refer to this as the store consciousness. What are contained in here are the various seeds to our moods and thought processes. Anger, hatred, desire, fear, love, compassion and all other emotions have their roots in this place. Some are watered and flourish, while others are not. Effort and guidance is required to change which seeds are targeted, but it is not entirely necessary to confront incestuous desires in order to do so.

The splitting of knowledge into different fields through the sciences and the lack of any wisdom tradition in the modern world can also help explain the growth of interest in Buddhism that has developed. People seem to have an inbuilt respect for this form of knowledge that deepens with time. In most cultures the image of the wise old man is heavily ingrained but lacks all credibility in the modern understanding of knowledge. While it diversifies and splinters over time his is supposed to reach a uniformity and simplicity that can be communicated directly and straightforwardly. New research, however, seems to vindicate this ancient image. It would appear that as we get older the brains pattern recognition ability becomes more pronounced, developing in each of us what is commonly known as wisdom. If this were to be joined with practises such as the Buddha-Dharma it could resurrect the image of the wise old man, full of knowledge and understanding. In fact, many Buddhist teachers are perfect examples of this stereotype. Zen (a highly Spartan form of Buddhism) abbots are rumoured to be the ultimate know-it-all's. Those who consider this strange could compare it to many current understandings of old age as both a painful process and burden on others and decide which they find more attractive. It must be remembered that throughout most of human history the old have been revered and respected because of their experience and insight. These new views of them and the sense of dislocation many older people feel because of them is a relatively recent phenomenon.

The practise of the Buddha-Dharma also forms a place of quietness in modern life that is very much lacking in the modern world. When the Buddha lived, and today, entering into the path was known as taking refuge. What this meant was taking refuge from the suffering and turmoil caused by unenlightened living. The Buddha and his teachings were a place of complete rest and acceptance, without any of the egotism, chaos and destruction that blights life. With the fast pace of modern life, tragic news stories all over television, unchecked military action in parts of the world and even the aggressive and devious nature of politics the existence of a refuge such as this can sometimes feel impossible to reach.

The modern search for external recognition and admiration to create existential justification has reached such a high point because of the lack of any other commonly accepted method to measure ourselves. How popular, wealthy or respected we are often becomes peoples only method of gauging their sense of self worth. Through practising the Buddha-Dharma a new basis and standard for judging the worthiness of life becomes open. Some will dislike such a measure, if only because it is not immediately clear to everyone around them and will probably not incur the jealousy of others. By being a basis for self worth, however, it provides a new source of self esteem that does not require the fluctuating and fleeting judgements or approvals of others. This latter model has been the cause of much desperate behaviour, as people find the most inappropriate sources to make themselves feel needed or wanted. Often it has involved the adoption of some form of pseudo-identity to attract attention from others. In other cases people have looked to indiscriminate sex or status within respected social groups to develop and maintain their sense of self worth and justification.

The acceptance of death and other realities that can be painful to contemplate can be reached through practising the dharma as well. What has become almost taboo to talk about in the Western world becomes the starting point of the Buddhist path. Not only is acknowledging these factors of life encouraged by the path, but keeping them constantly in mind is. They are removed from being locked into collective repression to being appreciated.

Rene Descartes is the philosopher who famously said 'I think, therefore I am'. This statement went on to shape the very formation and character of Western philosophy. It created what is known as the Cartesian split, a divide that is today manifested between mind and matter. Along the axis of matter we find what is measurable, impersonal, purposeless and value free. Due to the growth of science and its reliance upon all of the characteristics of this tangent this is the one that dominates our modern worldview. It is considered more real than what lies along the other tangent, which includes subjectivity, what is personal, volition, purpose and values. The scientific inability to pigeon hole the mind means that it has become the ignored side of the Cartesian split. These things that shape it are considered illusory at best. The Buddha's explanation of the mind and its relation to the world around it has the potential to change this. By taking the mind and its place in the world seriously this split could be closed and a more holistic world view could be opened up. With it, religion and philosophy in general can re-emerge as valid areas of life. Science, therefore, as it should provide us with how and the Buddha balances this out with explaining why.

Already in the West the numbers of those involved in Buddhist movements or practises has reached great numbers. Estimates have spread between America and Europe a number in the millions and it has been recorded as the fastest growing religion in Australia. Considering that Buddhism has only been taken seriously in the West in the past few decades this is a considerable number. The growing size of Buddhist sections in book shops and libraries testifies to this growth of interest and practise.

The real test of its application in the modern world, for those curious, can only be in the experiences and changes that these people report. The advantages they feel are probably a mix of those that are mentioned earlier and ones at a much more personal level. While some would find their decision hard to understand and perhaps odd, others could respond by pointing out how natural religion has always been to humanity and how some may feel a life without it is deeply lacking.

On this level Buddhism, if accepted, can fill the holes of nihilism and existential angst by providing a transcendent meaning in life. This is a field that has been studied more by Doctor Victor Frankl than most people. Frankl survived the Holocaust and attributed this to his belief in life's higher meaning and purpose. He had watched men who gave up on such a thing succumb to the death camps around him. His life's work as a psychiatrist centred on what he called logo-therapy. This is a branch of psychiatry that helps people find a higher meaning in their lives when they have lost all such motivation. Many people, without belief in a higher purpose around them, do not feel as if they can justify day to day life. Frankl saw the belief in meaning as the essential difference between those who survived the horrors of the concentration camps and those who did not.

 Unlike the nominal Christianity that sits in the background of so many peoples lives Buddhism provides a tradition which they can explore and delve into. Instead of the social obligation that religion has become for many, some desire to search for deeper and more meaningful answers and experiences. Going to church or service once a week hardly reaches into or fulfils the vast resources of spirituality that have been intertwined with so much of human history. If to yearn for this is as natural to humanity as it appears then not having this need satisfied could result in a feeling of deep inner loss. If it is true that some people are more religious in character than others, then the more so for them.

 Mihaly Csikszentmihalyi has spent his life researching what he calls flow. This is the state of mind reached when an individual is so immersed in a task they think of nothing else, forgetting all that they usually worry about. This state of immersion is experienced by everyone when they are absorbed in activities they care deeply about. Artists and athletes often talk about how their perception of time and space alter when they enter into this state of high focus, creativity and joy. Csikszentmihalyi has written about how certain personalities appear to better at conjuring this state of mind than others and so enjoy fuller lives. He also goes far to point out how subjective experience is not just a part of our lives but is our lives. Taking control of our subjective interpretation is taking control of the world we inhabit. It would seem as if he was aware that it took a lot for many people to realise how deeply true this was. So many have mistaken their interpretation for reality as the real thing, in a kind of naïve realism, they trap themselves inside it The similarity between this state of flow and what Buddhist practitioners seek is illuminating . Perhaps flow is one of the inherent qualities of nirvana.

Adopting the dharma as a meaning in life does not require revolution, violence or the radical challenging of the lives of others but a change in our perceptions of ourselves and the world. The other changes in life caused by the dharma gradually follow from this one. In this sense it is possible for anyone to take part at any position in life. Critics will say it is just another false religion, another crutch for the weak, but a deeper look at its relationship to other religions can help us understand its true worth.

It is not rare to hear people say things like 'if there were no religion there would be no war', or 'it would have been better if religion had never have been invented'. They look at the history of conflict in the world and decide that religion is the main motivating factor. Each creed attempts at various times to impose its belief upon others and stamp out rival world views. Often they take wars afflicting the world today as evidence of this hypothesis, thereby ignoring the deeper complexities of such conflict. How can any religion be true anyway, when they disagree with one another so deeply they ask? Anthropologist Stephen Oppenheimer has mentioned that it appears to be a deeply ingrained habit in humanity to emphasis the differences between ourselves and others as much as possible. One of the area's he mentions as evidence of this is the exaggeration of the differences between different religious traditions. Muslims, Christians, Jews, Hindu's and Buddhists are seen to psychologically inhabit incompatible worlds. Each claims their world is the only true one and all others are mistaken. In this sense this book is advocating the Buddhist world view over all others because it is right and all the others are wrong. These misconceptions are emphasised in the West by the highly exclusivist nature of Christian doctrine. Other religious followings are much more subtle in their relation to and understanding of other faiths. At the core of each of them can be found similar experiences and goals, only appearing superficially different because of how they grew in isolation to each other and within different cultural contexts. By looking at some of the details surrounding the formation of different world religions and finding similarities it can give some credence to the place of religious belief and spiritual practise in life. The Buddha described his path as making clear the central goal of all religions so there should be at least some account within each faith of the type of experiences he described.

 Those who dismiss religion entirely see it as an archaic method of trying to describe the world that no longer should be given any validity or have any place. There is good reason today to doubt this analysis and accept religion as a natural, perhaps even necessary, element of human life. In this sense it as normal behaviour and drive as sex but, just like sex, a life time repressing it will bring about forms of perversion. Perhaps political ideology could be included in this category. It would also mean that a world without religion is about as realistic as a world without sex. Just like everything else, however, there can be good religion and bad religion and too much of what people are aware of today is that which belongs firmly in the bad category. It is only because the good side is quieter by its very nature that there is less awareness of it and the influence it plays.

 Jonathan Haidt has put forward an interesting analysis of the role of religion in human life. He describes us as being surrounded by a higher dimension that is not within our logical or rational ability to grasp, just as in the same way as it wouldn't be possible for a two dimensional being to understand or conceptualise a third dimension. We can only intuit this dimension and sometimes vaguely sense its interaction within our perception of the world. Where religion comes in is as an artistic attempt to help us understand and live in harmony with this higher dimension. In this sense religious doctrine and belief should never be interpreted literally or absolutely but as a pointer towards a higher truth, impossible to describe in words. This is the dimension our sense of moral worth and value is intuited from. With this understanding Haidt lost the contempt for religion he held as a young scholar and realised its importance in terms of human development. Upon this dimension we exist on a scale with only ourselves aware of how far up or down this scale we are placed. When we act in harmony with this dimension and move up this scale the resulting feeling is often described as both enjoyable and meaningful. This is the feel-good factor exploited every Red Nose Day. This feeling of elation connected to ethical acts and characteristics is now being recognised and put under research. It is often felt as warmth or a glowing feeling in the chest and until recently little was said of this experience that most people are aware of.

Paths such as the Buddha's trace out the behaviour needed to make our way up this scale. Perhaps what he described as nirvana is its very apex. Haidt realised that his scale analogy revealed an ancient truth that usually only the most devoutly religious people grasp; that by our actions and thoughts we move up and down a higher dimension. Herein lies the core of all religion. Good religion is that which raises us up the scale, and bad that which stagnates us at one point or causes us to slide down. Sudden appreciations or lurches into this dimension are what is described as religious experience and are usually life changing. Normally an individual will interpret this through there own cultural lenses, and so you have people talking of Jesus entering into their hearts or finding God. Although he would not place the title God upon this dimension Haidt could easily accept the term divinity for it.

The image of Islam in the West has been damaged greatly by the work of a militant and destructive minority. The values this minority have displayed to the world are often taken as being representative of the tradition they have emerged from. Little has been said of the particularly Western roots of their world view. The writings of the founders of political Islam show more influence from older Western philosophers, such as Nietzsche, than they do from anything in Muslim history. The philosophy motivating suicide killings and acts of random violence seems to stem from the structure of Western ideological thought than anywhere else. The future Islamic state is the new utopia and Islamic law will be the rules that are to govern it. Of course, it can only be brought about through the use of apocalyptic violence and revolution. Many of the adherents of this fantasy are born among Muslim communities here in the West too parents who were prepared to accept secular society. It is likely the source for Islamism can be found in the existential boredom and nihilism afflicting youth in the West in general, rather than anything particular in the Muslim tradition. For these individuals this meaninglessness and emptiness can be cured by immersing themselves in what they feel to be a true representation of their heritage. That it is more akin to failed secular and Western ideological projects is probably not something that is raised much in fundamentalist Muslim circles. If political Islam is to be rooted out in the West it is through the active promotion of more accurate and authentic transmissions of the faith.

In the year 610 an Arab business man called Muhammad ibn Abdallah made his annual retreat during Ramadan, just outside the economically thriving city of Mecca. While Muhammad was growing up there had been a spiritual crisis in the Arabian Peninsula. A sense of spiritual inferiority had grown among them when they compared themselves to their Christian and Jewish neighbours. These people had a history of spiritual revelation and inspired scriptures they claimed came from God. Why, many of Muhammad's contemporaries wondered, had the divine never revealed itself to them? Although they did have their own religious traditions, many felt that they were no longer applicable to modern life. Mecca was the centre of the local pagan traditions of the time and had thrived because of it. The Arabs were split at this time between tribes and survived on a basis of blood vendetta. Should a person murder a member of one tribe anyone would do from their tribe to balance out the crime. Rules had been formed forbidding violence in Mecca, making it a safe haven for trade and interaction. Muhammad's own tribe, the Qurayesh, had grown rich and successful because of this geographical truce.

Something was to happen, however, during this years Ramadan retreat that was going to change all of this. While in the mountains outside Mecca Muhammad had the first of a series of experiences that would inspire and give him the strength to change everything about how the Arabian Peninsula was structured. A power overcame him and he felt compelled to recite words that captured the meaning of his experience. This first encounter with the divine is described as being orchestrated by the angel Gabriel, a figure that is usually used to represent divine truth. To begin with Muhammad attempted to hide what had happened, afraid that he would be thought of as a charlatan or mad. Eventually, with the support of those around him who discovered what was happening, he felt he had to preach about what he was going through and what it meant. These recitations would be compiled and became what is known today as the Koran.

The Sword From The Scabbard

Unlike traditions further East encountering the divine has often been a shocking or heavy experience for the monotheistic prophets. The ancient prophets of Israel had often felt it as a terrible burden when it revealed itself to them suddenly. It may be that the contemplative and meditative nature of the East better prepares people for the radically different nature of this layer of reality. Or perhaps also that the intensity of some peoples ability to interact with it can be too much for them. For Muhammad the sheer power of these experiences appears to have been immense. Sometimes he would seem to suffer pain, sweat and even lose consciousness as a result of them. Throughout his life not even his enemies would ever accuse him of faking what he was going through.

His encounters led him to see the way in which humanity was meant to live and interact with the divine. It differed quite a bit from the money hungry and tribal ethos that had grown throughout Arabia, Muhammad would have noticed. To the displeasure of his own tribe and others who had grown rich over the past few years, Muhammad began to preach his message in Mecca. Muhammad never thought of his message as an abnegation of any previous belief or faith but as the continuation of true faith. Just as the Buddha did, he believed he had rediscovered a way of life that was natural to humanity but had been lost in time. His teachings set out a series of rules that where designed to refine the individual, purifying them with this divine reality he referred to as Allah. The name he eventually came to for his movement was Islam, which means surrender. The believer was required to surrender their egotistical and self centred selves to this higher reality, thereby living in harmony with it.

The growing obsession with money and trade had to be challenged or greed would tear the entire peninsula apart. Something transcendent had to be placed in the centre of life before this happened and Muhammad was now convinced that Allah must be this centre. With this in mind he entered into a course of action that would result in him having to escape Mecca but return to it years later having gained support and changed the course of history.

Compared to most of the other world religious traditions, Islam is relatively young, so there is more detail available concerning its foundations. By the time his mission was over Muhammad had changed the religious and socio-political structures of his entire society. He had united the factions of Arabia into a new kind of super-tribe and steered them away from the greed and destruction that had previously made their lives so difficult. As an historical figure Muhammad is probably one of the most extraordinary individuals to ever live. For one person to implement such lasting changes so quickly is astounding. The emphasis upon charity, compassion and devotion in the movement he founded are reflections of qualities he displayed throughout his life. The detailed information from his biographies often display a character much more human than the founders of other religious movements and probably because of this much more likeable. That the movement he founded is now the world's fastest growing religion should not turn out, as so many fear, to be a bad thing.

In 632, with his many adventures over him and society forever transformed Muhammad died. He had complained of pains in his head for some time and rested it on his wife, Aisha's, lap. She knew he had finally died when she felt the weight of his head grow heavier on her legs. Some feared the community would not survive his death but it has. He had single-handedly brought peace to a war torn part of the world and changed all of the political and social traditions of his time for the better.

One of the stories about Muhammad's mystical encounters involves Gabriel coming for him and ascending with him up a ladder to the divine sphere and there they behold a 'nameless splendour'. This is the legendary Night Journey, the most famous and important point of Muhammad's internal experiences. Gabriel, the bearer of divine truth, takes him to see the celestial realm and he realises its indescribable nature. Later members of the Islamic community would try and emulate this internal spirituality and form a movement devoted to the way in which Muhammad interacted with the divine. These would be known as the Sufi's. Allah was to be found through an interior act of surrender. The self was to be pealed away layer after layer and Allah was to be discovered underneath. The similarities between this experience and the Buddha's description of true spirituality are unmistakable. Yazid al-Bistami in 874 taught that through this method an act of perfect Islam was possible. Surrendering to the divine completely and abandoning the self allows immersion into Allah therefore making man become divine. He understood this mystical journey to be a natural part of all our lives and communing with Allah to be what gives life meaning.

In Jewish circles the divine became anthropomorphised into God. This is what led to the Christian concept of the divine having a personality with thoughts and desires. Although some lament this turn because of the way in which it seems to justify the projection of human needs and wants onto the divine, there is some wisdom behind it. Humanity is the most complicated thing we are aware of and since the divine is greater than us it must be even more so. Anthropomorphism is a way of saying that the divine can never be any less than human. God, in Judaism, was to be cultivated from within, not thought of as a distant and judgemental watcher.

The reputation Jews have had because of the bad publicity Christianity gave them has tarnished them in the eyes of many. Ignorance still abates about their beliefs and practises and concepts of the divine. Many Christian's, instead of being respectful to their parent faith, still believe it to be a primitive and redundant version of Christianity. The treatment of the Jewish race throughout recent Western history has been disgraceful and there is no doubt these views of them has played its part.

It would appear that this is partly due to the easiness with which Christians have been able to project their own fears and insecurities onto others. It is similar to how the Muslims were perceived, during the Crusades, as a religion of the sword, when such a description would have been better suited to Christians of the time. Perhaps the image of God only being purely good has made it difficult for them to handle badness in themselves or connected to themselves. This results in projection of it onto the 'other'. Certainly the strangely hideous creation that is the Devil and some of the ridiculous beliefs concerning the Jews would appear to confirm such a hypothesis.

The idea of God having a personality, however, is still not as pronounced here as in Christianity. Instead Jewish conceptions of the ineffable are closer to Islamic views. This version of God definitely has 'ways that are not our ways'. Often some interpret that Christianity involves a defunct Jewish God being replaced by the purer Christian one. Jesus' life is the revelation of this new God to the world. As mentioned earlier closer analysis reveals the fundamentally Jewish nature of Jesus' teachings and belief. The story of Rabbi Hillel's golden rule is an example of both this and essentially good nature of Jewish teachings.

Kabala is the name usually given to the inner contemplative journey that is practised within Judaism. It is also worthy to note that that one of the acts of Jewish Throne Mysticism involved the practitioner resting his head down between his legs. Muhammad is recorded to also have adopted this position during some of his experiences, although he would never have known the Jewish mystics did the same.

Hinduism is the world religion with the most in common with Buddhism. No one is certain exactly when it dates from but it is accepted as the world's oldest surviving religious tradition. Its description of the mission of human life being absorption into something greater is similar to Buddhist understandings. Brahman is this divine reality and Atman the part of it that lies deep within ourselves. It would appear that many of the differences between it and the Buddha-Dharma lie in the use of terminology and symbology. The Buddha did not feel the eternal Self was a good description of the divine that lies within or that Brahmin was a good description of the divine outside. Throughout Hinduism there are millions of deities, each representative of this divine reality. By cultivating bhakti, devotion towards a deity, an individual could reach this kind of release by the manifestation of love and reverence. What appears to outsiders as a collection of idol type worshiping is actually a highly tolerant and ancient method of interacting with the divine. Although Christian missionaries have made gains in Africa and Asia, they have barely made a dent in the Hindu world. Its high regard for variety has meant a religion that only believes itself to be true has not found fertile ground for growth.

Taoism is centred around an ineffable force that flows through reality. This indefinable power is balanced delicately throughout the world, a status represented by the famous yin-yang symbol. When we are tuned into this force we become harmonised with the world around us and become as we are supposed to be. When we are out of tune with the Tao life can become chaotic and miserable. The rituals and teachings of Taoism try to mentally prepare the practitioner for intuiting this layer of reality. Often it involves putting our own small concerns out of the way by emptying our minds and feeling a greater force at work in our lives.

All of these terms and descriptions of the divine and the methods taught to interact with it have enough in common with each other to indicate that they are each referring to the same reality. No tradition realises this deeper than Hinduism, with its attitude of one truth but many descriptions. Of course, some will disagree and hold that their God is not the one encountered by other religions because they do not posses an adequate belief system. It is views like this, however, that are the cause of the disfavour held towards religion today. All of these traditions emphasis the battle against our own small ego and its selfish desire's in order to discover a deeper and truer force at work in the world. When we encounter and tune into this our lives become enriched and meaningful but without it they are sorely lacking in direction and drive. A real meaning in life should then be one which brings us into interaction with this reality and away from delusions.

In the past this may well have been provided by Christianity. Jesus' teachings do encourage believers to find the Kingdom of God within themselves and the devotion and love held towards God and Jesus could also be understood as a form of bhakti. An indication such an inner journey was practised by early Christians can be found in the story of Mary and Martha. In *Luke 10*, Jesus enters into the house of Martha and her sister Mary but while Martha is busying herself with work and serving Mary simply sits with Jesus and listens to him talk. Martha complains to Jesus but he explains to her how she is focused on unimportant things while Mary is doing all that is really necessary. This can be understood as Jesus giving his support to the contemplative tradition and its meditative path rather than pure service and work. That this story is not remembered in such a way sits well with the obsession with keeping busy and the external focus of Christianity and Western culture.

The connection between Christianity and this inner experience of the divine was jeopardised for Western Christians after the Reformation and the resulting wars concerning conceptual beliefs. Direct experience of the divine realm would never grow to hold the same place in Western Christianity as it did in all other religious traditions.

There are some thinkers who have even mentioned the possibility that Jesus, himself, may have been influenced by Buddhist or Hindu philosophy since in his time the lucrative Silk Route was open through Asia. Even Nietzsche described Jesus' mission as a kind of Buddhistic peace movement, that had been misunderstood by his peers. Some have put forward the suggestion that Christianity today should be mixed with Buddhist beliefs, in order to produce a religion that is true but also has Western grounding. The problem with this being that Jesus was not a Buddha and he did not teach what we know as Buddhism. Creating an amalgamation like this feels as if it is paving the way for another collapse.

The advent of the Enlightenment, as we have seen, made Christianity impossible to fully accept, so any chance of it connecting us through belief to the divine was vastly reduced. Instead, the ideologies rose to try and give new meaning to life, but without any reference or attempt to reach into divinity they were destined to inevitable collapse.

Buddha, Muhammad, Lao Tzu and the Jewish prophets were more concerned with our behaviour than with our beliefs. Since it was this which would determine whether our character was capable or not of reaching spiritual enlightenment it received the majority of focus. Beliefs of the conceptual mind were no more than symbols for something that could never be adequately described. By engaging with these symbols it is possible to encounter this reality, but mistaking these symbols for this reality makes such a thing impossible. Doing this is what we now refer to as religious fundamentalism. Theology and religious beliefs, then, is pure poetry and should be approached as such.

Karen Armstrong is the scholar who put forward the compassion induced altered state of consciousness hypothesis. She has put the motivation behind all of these traditions as an attempt to create a new kind of human being that transcends the egotistical and destructive creatures that too many people become. Or an attempt to curb the murderous instinct that seems to grip so many of us throughout history. This may sound idealistic or naïve but is a good bit more realistic than the utopia's that was once suggested to solve all such problems through political reorganisation.

In today's world the same old themes reappear in the form of modern mythologies. Religious fundamentalism, by the way, would be the equivalent of taking these stories literally. In the past mythology was used as a tool within religion to display values and spread correct understanding in the various traditions. The huge popularity, success and fan base's of series such as *The Lord of the Rings* or *Harry Potter* shows the human thirst for these kinds of big stories. In them good and evil are clearly defined for us and a deciding battle between them is fought. The central elements, themes and imagery of these epics are drawn from all of the world religions and reused skilfully. Much has been already written concerning the Catholic theology underpinning *The Lord of the Rings* and comparing Frodo's struggle with Christ's or the messiah status of Harry Potter and the use of resurrection imagery during his final battle with his arch-enemy Voldemort, but one franchise that does deserve deeper mention for its use of ancient philosophy and mythological elements is *Star Wars*.

Through it, director and writer, George Lucas has managed to boil down almost every world religion into its simplest format. The universe is controlled and infused by a divinely powerful element known as the Force. All things are joined by it and each priest (Jedi) must learn to live with it and work through it. The entire series involves just about every kind of miracle and theme recorded in human religious history. Virgin birth, messiah figures, wise old teachers, corruption, loss of faith, love, hatred and redemption are all tackled in its six part structure. In it a battle is fought between the Jedi and the evil Sith over control of the galaxy.

The story pivots around a messiah figure called Anakin Skywalker who becomes corrupted and joins the Emperor, the stories main villain. Lucas has even included references to Nietzschian philosophy, in that the Emperor is driven only by his greed for and worship of power. Anakin's decision to join the Emperor only results in his own self destruction and a weak servitude to him. Eventually, however, Anakin's son grows up and causes his father to redeem himself by destroying the Emperor and freeing the galaxy. It's only a pity the acting's so bad. There is no aspect of ancient mythology

The Sword From The Scabbard

Lucas has not touched upon here. Even the Catholic Church in Mexico thought so, when they attempted to sue him for copyright infringement.

The Matrix trilogy also reaches deeply into mythological and religious themes to structure itself. The first part, especially, is obvious in its portrayal of Buddhist death and enlightenment with Neo having to learn to see through the Matrix. With Agent Smith as Satan and Morpheus as John the Baptist the stage is also set for the martyring of Neo in a purely Christian fashion. Either way, just as in the major religious traditions, a death of the self is required to reach the final goal that is sought by the hero.

The original use for mythology as a vehicle of transmitting information necessary to live a full life may not be being used here completely. That does not mean, however, that people are not still impressed and influenced by these stories and the values they espouse. In fact, by the size of the interest in background information and stories it would appear instead that many are. They do seem to speak to a part of us that is just designed to receive and be moved by these kinds of stories, indicating that human beings, as well as being naturally religious are naturally mythological in nature.

Mythology has been astutely described as a kind of ancient method of psychotherapy and inner analysis. What is transmitted through it is the road that must be taken to reach maturity and enlightenment, along with warnings of what could lie down other paths.

As laid out by Joseph Campbell most mythologies are comprised of five parts. 1) The hero is called on a journey of some description. He may decline, but if he does this, although he will be safe, his life will not change. 2) A road of trials and challenges is raised. If he fails he may return or give up but if he succeeds he will reach a worthy goal. 3) He will receive the goal, which is normally always important self-knowledge. 4) He must attempt to return home, which he can still fail on. 5) He gets home and is able to apply the knowledge to the betterment of the world. Prometheus, Moses, Neo, Luke Skywalker, Harry Potter and all other hero's basically follow this same trajectory. Most cultures have their own version of what Campbell has called the *Hero of a Thousand Faces*. Unfortunately, in modern times these stories have become separated from their original meanings, although it is certain that Lucas was well aware of Campbell's work when he began writing his space opera.

Where the Buddha can come in is that his path truly does describe what lies at the heart of all these religions and mythologies. The Buddha went on his journey, endured the trials, discovered the goal and returned to teach it to the rest of the world. Now by teaching it he expects us to follow the same path. Instead of being confined to the realms of meaningless entertainment, modern mythologies could be used as they were meant to be and as their predecessors were designed to be used.

 Also, within his system of teachings there have been built safeguards against the emergence of religious fundamentalism and gross misunderstandings. Unlike other traditions, where encountering the divine has become obscured or misunderstood, his draws out the path to it clearly. Even those who retain faith in the traditions they were born into can still learn something from the teachings he left behind. The true differences between these religions appear to be mainly cultural and superficial in nature rather than doctrinal. The Buddha recognised the need for different methods of teaching among different people and did so in his own lifetime without jeopardising the core of his philosophy. By looking at some of his teachings the leaders and practitioners of other religions may be able to learn more about what their own traditions really mean.

 Other religious paths may have introverted methodologies but few count them as natural to humanity as Buddhism does. In the modern world, where we like to have something explained to us before we do it, the Buddha's life and teachings are perfectly suited. When we ask the Buddha why we shouldn't be selfish an immediate answer can be provided and explained rather than that it is against God's will or you won't get to Heaven if you are. The Buddha will answer that you will never be happy or complete if you are selfish, and will also be able to explain why this is.

CONCLUSION

At the beginning of this book I explained how it was set out to describe the process by which the sense of meaning in life had been taken from so many in the modern world. The cause of this, as I hope has been described clearly, was the collapse of Christianity in the face of the Enlightenment. Why it collapsed has to do with its unusual nature. In other words it was incompatible with reality. To understand this we had to examine its origins and the true reasons why it shaped out in the way it did.

The other issue we have looked at is how many of the attempted secular replacements of it have been no more than shallow corruptions of it and that many of the beliefs we still hold onto today, although many of us believe otherwise, are still entirely Christian derived. As such they have been unable to hold out against the same realities that brought down their source.

Nietzsche was brought into the book because of the way in which he saddles the era of total Christian belief and that of Christian rejection. The other important reason for his inclusion is because of his insight that now Christianity had given way, any new motivation in life had to come from entirely outside its world view. Mere corruptions or watered down versions of it could not do since they would be vulnerable to the same threats. History has proven him right. The various political ideologies caused mayhem before falling and modern secular society now displays a cynical tiredness about itself.

The second half has been spent trying to explain why, of all the traditions outside Christianity, Buddhism is the most appropriate for the modern condition. This is because it appears to be catered perfectly to the sense of disillusionment that has made its way into the heart of Western civilization. Its psychological and philosophical sharpness also means that it can stand the pressures of reasoned debate and analysis. It also forms a different world view and ethical standpoint to Christianity and so is not subject to the same type of criticism. The fact that it predates Christianity by several hundred years also means that it cannot be criticised as being some kind temporary fad but that it is here to stay.

The other reason why it is highly appropriate for practise in the modern age is that it is true. The collected scientific evidence recorded here may go some distance in support of this but ultimately it can only really be proven to any of us is through its individual application.

Another issue that has been touched upon here is that of what could be called the religious urge. While some secular thinkers have thought of religion as existing only in the conceptual mind the evidence from human behaviour and history seems to point otherwise. Human beings are highly religious creatures and will find satisfaction for this urge in one place in another. Many of the problems the world has faced have been caused by the pouring of religious energies into places that are just not designed to hold them.

What would it mean if it is true that religion is entirely natural to humanity? That a life ignoring it means a life repressing it, in the same way sex was once repressed in Western civilization and as we know, repression is never good. The time of the ideological perversions of this drive is over and early indications are that the new perversion of religious fundamentalism is set to take their place. As mentioned earlier, many scholars are predicting the rise of a post-secular age, so the real question to ask is what form of religiosity will grow to dominate this predicted age? Will it be the exclusivist and dogmatic versions that attract so much publicity today? If religion is permitted back into the public sphere to deal with this form of repression, as some suggest, will it only be in this small minded and damaging form? For those who find such a prospect disturbing, perhaps it is time the monopoly on religious belief and practise was removed from the hands of extremists and returned to moderate and progressive believers.

This could also result in the return of the study of religion and spirituality to the position of a highly respected practise. Perhaps then it could evolve beyond empty debates such as creation versus evolution or the historical validity of the Flood. Real research could be carried out into the best way for reaching the potential that religion is designed to activate, through the budding science of neurotheology. Or understand and develop the meanings of the various hagiographies and how they are supposed to relate to everyday life instead of the distant past. If the divine, as Haidt understood it, is real, then its importance to daily life is absolutely paramount. If it truly does infuse all of reality then ignoring it and trying to live without reference to it is deeply unwise. In fact it would mean that, as all religions do teach, it should be the central focus of life.

At the very least Buddhism provides a container for the religious urge that can manifest it as it is meant to be. Fundamentalist beliefs are not an element of its practise and it does not need major re-evaluation, as Christianity would, if it were to be accepted by more people in today's world. It strikes a middle way between extremities and has so far avoided many of the faults religion is generally accused of. Combined with the growing evidence in support of its truth, all of this makes it an attractive option. That is what I have tried to show in this book through an attempted explanation of the source of Buddhism and its nature. In support of this I have described some of the growing evidence in support of the Buddha's description of our place in reality and how especially applicable many of its features can be to modern life.

The Sword From The Scabbard

The fact remains that Christianity is still here to stay and no one is suggesting that Buddhism will ever replace it, but for Buddhist practitioners this is in no way a bad thing. The idea that everyone should be of the same religion is a monotheistic one, so conversion has never been an element of Buddhism. In fact it is normally discouraged because of the risk of misunderstandings and simplifying of beliefs and practises that can occur when too many people are involved. Some traditions actually discourage teaching until the potential student has pestered the teacher enough to prove their commitment.

In fact the only religion look set to truly challenge Christianity in the West is Islam. The growth in its Western community over the past few years is not surprising, given its greater acceptability within modern knowledge and lack of theological difficulty. It has more to stand on at its base than Christianity and so is surer of itself and its devotion to Allah. For those tired and disillusioned with secular replacements or the total repression of spirituality its single minded devotion to the divine is refreshing. Although it is designed for everyone in the same way Christianity was, it has never been as exclusivist in doctrine.

In the past where monotheistic religions have existed they have come to dominate the society and cultures they are a part of. In the modern West this is no longer possible. In many parts of the world it is now possible to gain information and knowledge on subjects our ancestors would never known existed. For Buddhists who could come to feel isolated in their practise in the West, on-line communities and forums now exist in order to share advice, knowledge and experiences between adherents. The image of one religion dominating the entire landscape is not one that is likely to return in the near future.

Many books concerning Buddhism are filled with quotations from intellectuals and thinkers commending the virtues of it and the Buddha himself. The contributors have ranged from Albert Einstein to Arnold Toynbee, but there is only one quote I want to include and it is because of the normally negative regard its source held thought systems other than his own.

The Sword From The Scabbard

Nietzsche recognised that Buddhism had the potential to offer Westerners new meaning in life since it lay outside all Christian contexts and was, as he saw it, mostly true. Compared to most other thinkers of his past, Nietzsche admired the Buddha and the nature of his teachings. Included with his usual Christianity bashing he wrote '...Buddhism is a hundred times more realistic than Christianity....it arrives after a philosophical movement lasting hundreds of years; the concept of 'God' is already abolished by the time it arrives. Buddhism is the only positivistic religion history has to show us, even in its epistemology (a strict phenomenalism -)..The precondition for Buddhism, is that it is the higher and even learned classes in which the movement has its home. The supreme goal is cheerfulness, stillness, absence of desire, and this goal is achieved. Buddhism is not a religion in which one aspires after perfection: perfection is the normal case.'

The Sword From The Scabbard

NOTES

CHAPTER 1

[The historicity of Jesus is an area that has been the result of extensive research and given birth to various theories and often colourful ideas. Most of the details given here, such as Jesus being a Pharisee, the real meaning of the term 'Son of God' and so on can be found covered well in Karen Armstrong's classic **A History of God.** A clear and concise description of the development of Christian doctrine and the rise of the church can be found in **Civilization: a New History of the Western World** by Roger Osborne.
]

CHAPTER 2

[Osborne's **Civilization** is also worthy for its coverage of the Dark Ages and the Renaissance that followed. **The Secrets of Happiness** by Richard Schoch covers the impact St. Thomas Aquinas had on Christianity. It also covers the lacking nature of modern conceptions of happiness. The developments from the Reformation to atheism can be found described clearly in **The Twilight of Atheism: The Rise and Fall of Disbelief in the Modern World** by Alastair McGrath. He also covers Paley, Darwin and the rise of atheism quite well. The modern nature of religious fundamentalism is explained in Armstrong's **The Battle for God: Fundamentalism in Judaism, Christianity and Islam.** To understand the rise of the ideologies as religious repression the work of John Gray the author of **Straw Dogs** and **Black Mass** is highly advisable.

Michael Burleighs writing is also advised, both **Earthly Powers** and **Sacred Causes.** It is he who points out clearly the distinction between world transcendent and world immanent religions.]

CHAPTER 3

[Edward Barnays effect on consumerist society is also explained in Osborn's **Civilization**. The figures concerning the revenue generated from self help books and anti-depressants can be found in Matthieu Ricards **Happiness: A Guide to Developing Life's Most Important Skill.** The issues of modern cynicism and neurosis are mentioned in **Going Buddhist** by Peter Conradi. The targeting of pre-schoolers by advertising agencies is covered in **Buy Baby Buy** by Susan Gregory Thomas. **Nietzsche: A Philosophical Biography** is good for those who wish to understand more about the 19th century philosopher and his work. The driving of consumer culture by counter culture is explained clearly in **The Rebel Sell** by Joseph Heath and Andrew Potter.]

CHAPTER 4

[Armstrong's **The Great Transformation: The World in the Time of Buddha, Socrates, Confucius and Jeremiah** is a great coverage of the Axial Age and what it means to us today. Another of her books is **Buddha**, which is a good introduction to the life, times and teachings of the Buddha.]

CHAPTER 5

[The importance of the discovery of neuroplasticity is described by Ricard in his book **Happiness**, along with descriptions of some of the work being done by the Life and Mind Institute and accounts of the experiments being carried out on experienced meditators. He also describes the difference between the part of the brain that deals with what is liked and what is wanted. The link between the parietal lobes and mystical states can be found in Jonathan Haidts **The Happiness Hypothesis**. Stephen Batchelor's

Buddhism Without Beliefs explains how Buddhism can be applied without the need for what is seen as superstitious beliefs. Glimpses into the work of Ian Stevenson can be found in collections of some of his cases such as **20 Cases Suggestive of Reincarnation** and **Where Reincarnation and Biology Intersect.** Tom Shroder's book **Old Souls** is a great outsider's perspective. As for the quantum revolution any book on the area of 'new science' should be enough to impress the reader with its strangeness. Paul Davies, however, is one of the most well recognised writers on the subject. His book **The Goldilocks Enigma** is especially good.]

CHAPTER 6

[**Straw Dogs** by John Gray mentions the modern obsession with distraction and Thich Nhat Hanh mentions how the idea of happiness can be a dangerous thing in **The Heart of the Buddha's Teachings**. The growth of wisdom in old age is the subject of the book **The Wisdom Paradox** by Elkhonon Goldberg. The book **Flow** by Mihaly Csikszentmihalyi covers its titular subject. The person today most associated with comparative religious study is Karen Armstrong and all of her books are worth reading. The fourth dimension description of religion is also included in Haidts **The Happiness Hypothesis** and Western philosophical influences on political Islam are also a part of Gray's book **Black Mass.**]